THE DEFICIT DELUSION

THE DEFICIT DELUSION

WHY EVERYTHING LEFT, RIGHT, AND SUPPLY-SIDE TELLS YOU ABOUT THE NATIONAL DEBT IS WRONG

JOHN TAMNY

Since 1947
REGNERY
An Imprint of Skyhorse Publishing, Inc.

Copyright © 2025 by John Tamny

All rights reserved. No part of this book may be reproduced in any manner without the express written consent of the publisher, except in the case of brief excerpts in critical reviews or articles. All inquiries should be addressed to Regnery, 307 West 36th Street, 11th Floor, New York, NY 10018.

Regnery books may be purchased in bulk at special discounts for sales promotion, corporate gifts, fund-raising, or educational purposes. Special editions can also be created to specifications. For details, contact the Special Sales Department, Regnery, 307 West 36th Street, 11th Floor, New York, NY 10018 or info@skyhorsepublishing.com.

Regnery® is an imprint of Skyhorse Publishing, Inc.®, a Delaware corporation.

Visit our website at www.regnery.com.

10 9 8 7 6 5 4 3 2 1

Library of Congress Cataloging-in-Publication Data is available on file.

Cover design by David Ter-Avanesyan
Cover photo by Getty Images

Print ISBN: 978-1-5107-8485-7
Ebook ISBN: 978-1-5107-8488-8

Printed in the United States of America

For Bob Reingold, a great friend who is an even better thinker and advice giver.

Contents

INTRODUCTION   ix

CHAPTER ONE
They're All 30 Days from Bankruptcy, and Have No Debt   1

CHAPTER TWO
Not Just Any Government Can Run Up Debt   11

CHAPTER THREE
Let's Be Serious: Deficits Are NOT An Effect of Too Much Spending   23

CHAPTER FOUR
Government Debt Doesn't Cause "Inflation"   35

CHAPTER FIVE
Ronald Reagan's Tax Cuts Did Cause the Deficits,
but Not for the Reasons You've Been Told   49

CHAPTER SIX
No, Central Banks Cannot and Do Not Finance Governments   63

CHAPTER SEVEN
Government Spending Is the Biggest, Most Progress-Restraining
Tax of Them All   79

CHAPTER EIGHT
If the Middle Classes Were Expected to Pay Back the Debt,
There Would Be No Debt   97

CHAPTER NINE
Low-Birthrate Hand-Wringing Reveals the Latent Keynes
Within Economists   107

CHAPTER TEN
Whatever You Do, Don't Let the Deficit "Hawks" Reform Social
Security and Medicare! 117

CONCLUSION 131
ACKNOWLEDGMENTS 141
ENDNOTES 145
INDEX 155

Introduction

The ordinary must live in obedience and have no right to transgress the law, because they are, after all, ordinary. While the extraordinary have the right to commit all sorts of crimes and various ways to transgress the law, because in point of fact they are extraordinary.
—Fyodor Dostoevsky, *Crime and Punishment*, p. 259

It was fall of 2024, and the race for the White House was in full force. Donald Trump vs. Kamala Harris, and with national elections of recent vintage frequently coming down to just a few votes either way, both candidates were feverishly trying to secure them everywhere they could possibly be found.

This rush for votes manifested itself in a number of ways, including with promises of tax cuts. As a front-page story in the *Wall Street Journal* described it, Trump and Harris were bringing "a whole new meaning to free-market economics," but not of the noninterventionist kind. Instead, the candidates were said to be "promising voters everything but the kitchen sink" when it came to tax cuts. There would be tax-free overtime pay, no tax on tips, tax-free Social Security income, along with free home healthcare and free newborn expenses.

About all the promises, University of California, Berkeley, economist Alan Auerbach observed rather dyspeptically that "We seem to be having an arms race. It's emblematic of the complete breakdown of any kind of responsibility about the budget."[1] Ah yes, the budget. And an allegedly looming crisis related to it.

While politicians can be expected to offer all manner of so-called "giveaways" every election cycle, pundits and economists can be expected to pour cold water on the very notion of reducing the federal government's share of wallet. To economists and the pundits who read economists, "crisis" of a too-much-debt kind always and everywhere awaits due to the "generosity" and prodigality of the political class.

What's interesting about this viewpoint is that it's both constant in the fusillade of alarmist commentary sense, but also monolithic. The fear of what awaits us owing to the $36 trillion debt has bipartisan qualities. This is true even during election periods.

Holman Jenkins is the *Wall Street Journal*'s libertarian-leaning "Business World" columnist, and arguably the most prominent business columnist in the world. Writing in October 2024, a little less than a month before voters went to the polls, Jenkins wrote in sober fashion "that another pending crisis, the fiscal unraveling of U.S. and other Western welfare states, eventually will revive bipartisan interest" in finding new sources of tax revenue.[2]

On the other side of the ideological spectrum, an editorial in the *Washington Post* lamented Donald Trump's "tax and spending proposals" that would allegedly "increase primary deficits." Getting right to the point, the *Post*'s editorial board asserted à la Jenkins that "Figuring out how to raise more tax revenue" will be a "central task" for future policymakers given the newspaper's broad view that "THE NATION faces a fiscal reckoning."[3]

Left and right, but largely the same views about deficits and debt: that a crisis awaits owing to it. One guesses that the *Post*'s editorial board would even jump on Jenkins's longtime support for a carbon tax as a way to raise the tax revenues thought to be necessary to pay off the debt. Supply-siders would of course not agree with the left or right on what's required to avoid an alleged "fiscal reckoning," but much like them, supply-siders similarly share their view that deficits can be solved by raising the amount of dollars the U.S. Treasury takes in.

Bringing the debt and deficit discussion even closer to the present day, with the inauguration of Donald Trump as the United States' 47th president on January 20, 2025, so began a valiant effort by the world's richest man, Elon Musk, to substantially reduce the size and cost of the federal government. He called his initiative "DOGE," or Department of Government Efficiency.

Notable about Musk's surely aggressive approach to shrinking government was the underlying narrative that informed his efforts. Musk felt he was doing the crucial work of helping the United States avoid a crisis. In his words, "We simply cannot sustain as a country $2 trillion deficits. Just the interest on the national debt now exceeds the Defense Department's spending. If this continues, the country will become de facto bankrupt."[4]

On the subject of deficits and debt, nothing changes. Alarmism, varying solutions born of alarmism, inevitably followed by more deficits and debt. Members of the left think the debt can be solved with more "taxes on the rich" in concert with so-called "entitlement reform," right- and libertarian-leaning scolds tell us the debt can be fixed with a combination of spending cuts, entitlement reform, and tax increases, while supply-side happy talkers claim the debt can be erased through tax cuts that shower politicians with even more tax revenue. The simplistic solutions raise a delicate question about whether left, right, and supply side have even a faint clue about what they're arguing.

Which is the point of this book. They're all wrong. And they're wrong regardless of whether you the reader think deficits and debt are a big problem, a big yawn, or something in between. Better yet, the various ideologies have no chance of ever solving what is or is not (depending on your view of government) a problem precisely because they don't understand why there are deficits and debt in the first place. *The Deficit Delusion* aims to fill in this cavernous hole of misunderstanding, but to do so it's essential to digress. And travel back in time.

* * *

In February 2011 venture capitalist Bill Gurley and Benchmark Capital paid $12 million to Uber in return for a 20 percent stake in the then largely unknown start-up.[5] While in 2025 Uber is one of the few companies in the world that can claim noun, verb, and adjective status, back in 2011 cofounder Travis Kalanick had to accept a term sheet that handed over a sizable portion of the nascent ride-sharing service to Benchmark.

It raises an obvious question that some might view as flippant, and that still others might view as obtuse: why on earth did Uber give so much of itself away in return for so little? More important, why didn't Uber just borrow $12 million rather than sell so much of its bright future away so cheaply? Uber was and still is transformative in the lives of people the world over. Thanks to the San Francisco–based company, customers can now summon a ride all day and every day to basically anywhere.

As is so often true of entrepreneurs, the advances they *lead* empower the common man and woman to act like *very rich* common men and women. Let's refer to ride-hailing as the twenty-first-century version of the proverbial bell that the well-to-do of old could ring to summon help from the servant, butler, and yes, the driver. What an advance Uber has overseen. From there, consider the possibilities.

In considering them, think about Amazon. Those who became familiar with the "Everything Store" first got to know it as a *bookstore* in the 1990s. That is, assuming they'd heard of it. It's so easy to forget how outré Amazon's conceit once was. Selling books "online"? Easily forgotten too is how very outside the norm *online* was not terribly long ago.

As Jimmy Soni wrote in his 2022 book about the creation of PayPal, *The Founders*, "In the late 1990s, only 10 percent of all online commerce was conducted digitally—the vast majority of transactions still ended with a buyer sending a check by mail."[6] Stop and think about that. It wasn't terribly long ago that we paid the bills, and for all manner of other things, with the USPS as the carrier of the check used to complete the transaction. Yet Jeff Bezos thought people would buy books in a way they never had before. No checks in the mail required, credit cards on the "internet" required. Call this a heavy lift.

Yet Bezos saw books as just the beginning. If he could convince the buying public to see the genius of book buying on their computers in replacement of the traditional bookstore, think of the myriad other ways that consumers could transfer their shopping habits to the then largely unknown internet. Think indeed. For a long time Amazon was a bit of a joke, or the punchline ("Amazon.org") for internet companies that were long on wild-eyed hype, but rather short when it came to turning profits.

Amazon is a useful way of considering Uber and its founders handing over 20 percent of the company in return for $12 million. And it helps explain why the founders eagerly exchanged so much equity for a relatively small amount of capital. The answer is that few expected Uber would make it. This includes Benchmark Capital. No doubt Kalanick and his fellow opposite thinkers had designs on applying the ride-hailing notion to all sorts of services not related to rides (the Amazon of transportation), but in 2011 they still had to convince not just those in need of a ride to summon one on an app, but they also had to convince individuals who happened to own cars to turn their mode of transportation into a business. Which requires a pause on the way to answering the question about why Uber exchanged equity for capital rather than debt.

In considering Uber's seemingly noneconomic choice of equity finance over debt, it's useful to think about entrepreneurs for a little bit. And in thinking about them, it's useful to contemplate the various university programs in the United States and around the world that offer college majors focused on entrepreneurship.

On its face, what a positive sign. There's so much criticism of colleges and universities right now, there's so much in the way of criticism of these institutions of higher learning as hotbeds of anti-capitalist hate,[7] yet they offer a great deal of instruction on the matter of entrepreneurialism. Really, what could be more capitalistic than inventing the commercial future as entrepreneurs have done, and continue to do? Universities are instructing their students on how to lead customers to wants that they never knew they had. Or are they?

The question is asked when it's remembered that in thinking about what entrepreneurs have done and will do, it's easy to see that "majoring in entrepreneurialism" is a blinding contradiction. There's quite simply no way to major in entrepreneurialism, period. Write this truth down over and over again.

There's no way to major in entrepreneurialism simply because the latter isn't a choice, or a subject, as much as it's a *state of mind*. Entrepreneurs don't choose their lot in life. Seriously, who would choose a commercial path littered with massive skepticism from the best of the best in business, ridicule from the best of the best in business, and then as Uber reminds us, financing from investors who, as evidenced by how much of your business concept they're demanding in return for money, are almost as skeptical about your chances of success as those showering you with skepticism and ridicule.

No one would choose the entrepreneurial path, simply because the true entrepreneur would find it impossible to not travel "off the beaten track," in the words of Fyodor Dostoevsky. The Dostoevsky quote that begins this chapter might be read by some as a comment on criminals, but the great nineteenth-century novelist was more realistically thinking about entrepreneurs who "have the gift or talent of speaking a *new word* in their environment."[8] In other words, they have something new to say, and that they *must* say. Still, saying what you believe in the face of ridicule is not for the faint of heart, which is why it's not a choice.

As Whole Foods cofounder John Mackey explained it in his 2024 memoir, *The Whole Story*, "It's not that I was trying to be a rebel; it's just that I couldn't conform."[9] *Exactly*. Applying for and securing a traditional job would have been an impossibility for Mackey. Same with starting a traditional grocery store. Mackey thought traditional grocery stores were doing it wrong, hence his desire to open Safer Way against all odds, and eventually Whole Foods.

Mackey observes about himself that "One of my superpowers is my evangelical enthusiasm,"[10] but in reality Mackey's true superpower is his contrarian view of business that he couldn't help expressing. Ask Mackey to extol the virtues of a typical Kroger or Safeway store, and it's a very safe bet that Mackey would be quite a bit less than evangelical, and by extension not in the least compelling.

Entrepreneurs quite simply *can't not do*, at which point they direct their energies toward concepts that are yet again well outside the norm to "move the world and lead it towards a goal." Entrepreneurs don't express a desire to "disrupt"; rather, their contrarian way of looking at how things are done has them passionately in favor of "destruction of the present in the name of the better."[11] It can't be stressed enough that the disruption isn't so much a choice or the objective as it is a consequence of a different, frequently very odd, "off the beaten track" state of mind.

Hopefully this helps readers better understand the *why* behind Uber selling 20 percent of itself for $12 million, as opposed to going into debt with a loan of $12 million. Or perhaps the digression into entrepreneurialism and what instigates it confuses the issue. Really, why would those so evangelical about their business concept exchange equity in return for cash in the first place? How contradictory it is to sell so cheaply what one believes in so deeply. And it's not just Uber. In 1988, Mackey and his investors sold 34 percent of Whole Foods equity in return for $4.5 million,[12] while in 1987 VC firm Sequoia Ventures secured 33 percent of Cisco Systems for $2.5 million.[13] Why are all these passionate doers willing to give up so much of what they're passionate about for so little?

Many readers know the answer to this ostensible riddle. Entrepreneurs exchange so much of what they believe in for very little simply because there's not an interest rate high enough to properly compensate investors for loaning money to entrepreneurial business concepts. As Sebastian Mallaby explained it in his 2022 history of the venture capital industry, *The Power Law*, most start-ups "fail completely."[14] And since most start-ups fail completely, a loan amounts to handing over cash in return for future income streams that most likely will never materialize. With start-ups, "future" and "income streams" are both extraordinarily unlikely.

Except that there's more. Consider the assessment of PayPal cofounder and venture capitalist Peter Thiel, an individual who famously exchanged $500,000 for 10.2 percent of Facebook back in 2003.[15] Whether he knows it or not, Thiel has a rather Dostoyevskian view of technology entrepreneurs, and long ago he expressed the belief to partners in his VC (Founders Fund) that "We should be more tolerant of founders who seem strange or extreme." Mallaby's assessment of how Thiel sees the start-up world is that the best founders are "arrogant, misanthropic, or borderline crazy."[16]

Notably, Thiel didn't just become a venture capitalist in pursuit of the odd. While it's easy to conclude that someone so close to technology was always aware that oddness and success weren't enemies (after all, he and Elon Musk built PayPal together!), Thiel and his partners passed on Uber and its cofounder after Kalanick "alienated" them. This led Thiel to conclude that "Maybe we need to give assholes a second and third chance."[17]

Bringing it back to debt, even though Thiel himself migrates toward the "strange or extreme," and not infrequently the "assholes," he's well aware that the oddballs he backs with investment will more often than not fail. He noted in his 2014 book *Zero to One: Notes on Startups, or How To Build the Future*, that "most venture-backed companies don't IPO or get acquired; most fail, usually soon after they start." Here, again, is the debt problem.

The very notion of debt in relation to entrepreneurs is an utter nonstarter. Debt is trust. When someone lends you money, there's an obvious expectation that the money be paid back. That's hardly an insight. The interest rate charged for the money loaned is the profit. As has been discussed, lenders don't have equity, hence the need for the loan to be paid back.

With start-ups, what's expected to die very quickly has very low odds of paying back funds borrowed. The previous truth requires a repeat of what was stated earlier: there's no interest rate high enough to compensate investors who would loan money to start-ups. Simple stuff. Which is a long way of answering the Uber riddle. No doubt Kalanick was confident that Uber would achieve great things, no doubt Kalanick was evangelical about Uber's prospects, but all entrepreneurs are evangelical, borderline crazy, occasionally sociopathic, and all sorts of other pejoratives. If they weren't, they wouldn't be entrepreneurs.

Uber exchanged 20 percent of its equity for $12 million simply because debt wasn't an option. Not even close. Silicon Valley is brimming with entrepreneurs with powerful visions of a future that in no way resemble the present. And because they believe as they do, most often they'll fail in pursuit of their opposite vision of how things should be. Change is hard.

Which leads to a seemingly obvious question. While readers might be able to accept the unwillingness of investors to lend money to entrepreneurs who much more often than not will fail completely very quickly, why would they back them at all? If there's no interest rate high enough to compensate a lender willing to back an entrepreneur, why would there be finance of any kind for the oddballs?

Venture capitalist legend Vinod Khosla provides the answer to the above question, or at least part of it. He observes that "Most people think improbable ideas are unimportant," which is why true entrepreneurs are such a rare breed. They're the "unreasonable" men and women who look at how things are—and that are making "most people" very happy—with haughty disdain. Which is why Khosla adds on to his comment about "improbable ideas" with the further assertion that "the only thing that's important is something that's improbable." What delights Khosla is when the "creatively maladjusted" bring him ideas that he deems *impossible*.[18]

"Impossible" is the answer to so many questions about oddball entrepreneurs. No doubt investments in the maladjusted and those "borderline crazy" or arrogant enough to think they can steer people away from the products and services they're rather satisfied with most often result in quick failure, but much less than very occasionally they succeed. And when they do, the payouts can be enormous.

Explained more simply, the business model of venture capitalists is to invest in businesses that will most likely fail. That is so because the proverbial singles or doubles when it comes to investing will in no way pay for copious failure in the space. Venture capitalists must back the impossible simply because when investments in the "impossible" actually succeed, the surprise is so great that the investment returns more than make up for all the failures they back.

Of course, the rare successes from impossible investments explain yet again why debt for start-ups is a nonstarter. Imagine risking millions with a loan to a company that's most likely to go under, only for that company to become a grand success. Imagine then only getting the money loaned in return for all the risk taken. No thanks. Such a loan would be incredibly exploitative, of the lender. With venture capital it's equity finance only. If it were debt, there quite simply would be no venture capital. The losses would far outpace the gains, and it wouldn't even be close.

Which brings us back to Uber. While Benchmark Capital's exchange of $12 million in return for 20 percent of Uber signaled a contradictory belief in the company's potential in concert with its likely failure, Uber, as most readers well know, succeeded. Big-time. By 2012 and 2013 it was already a verb and very much a "Unicorn." Unicorns are, like the eponymous creature, nearly mythical themselves because billion-dollar valuation start-ups are so rare. Again, if they weren't "unicorns," then they wouldn't be entrepreneurial ventures.

Uber had succeeded against all odds, and its valuation was zooming upward. In 2019 Uber IPO'd, or went public, and as of the writing of this book, it can lay claim to a market capitalization of *$157 billion*. Readers with a simple calculator can do the math on the returns achieved by Benchmark. A $12 million capital commitment would today be worth nearly *$30 billion* if Benchmark had held on to all its shares. It didn't, but that's not the point.

The point is that as evidenced by Uber's private valuation ($60 million) in 2011 relative to today, investors not only didn't expect Uber to make it, but they also hadn't much of a clue of how valuable Uber could eventually be. Markets are a look into the future, and if investors could have reasonably expected a $157 billion valuation in 2024, then it's no insight to point out that Benchmark couldn't have purchased its 20 percent stake for $12 million.

Put more bluntly, if it had at all been expected that Uber would become a $157 billion company, then it's a safe bet that it wouldn't have sold even one share in return for cash, let alone 20 percent of its shares. Evidence supporting this claim can be found in the fact that the Uber which sold 20 percent of itself for $12 million in 2011 can now lay claim to *$11 billion* worth of debt on its books.

What a change for the once expected-to-fail ride-hailing service. Formerly only able to sell large chunks of itself in return for cash, Uber can now issue debt. And lots of it.

At this point some readers are telling themselves that they purchased a book titled *The Deficit Delusion* in expectation of reading something full of graphs, equations, and percentages meant to explain the national debt in the United States. No thanks. Thousands of those books have been written, and tens of thousands more of those books will be written and published.

Without fail, the books on budget deficits, national debt, "Ponzi Schemes," and "unsustainable debt" will claim that a "debt crisis" of mythic proportions awaits us. It's an exaggeration for sure, but not much of an exaggeration, that a Rose Bowl or two could be filled with all the politicians, economists, and pundits who've predicted in the past, or are predicting now and in the future, a "debt crisis." Readers can rest assured they'll find none of that here. And to the extent that "debt crisis" will be mentioned in this book, it will be to mock the alarmists in our midst.

About this book's occasionally mocking tone, it should in no way be construed as an endorsement of all the federal debt, or an endorsement of government spending more broadly. Quite the opposite, particularly when it comes to government spending. The deeply held view here is that government spending is the most economy-sapping tax on freedom and growth of all, and nothing else comes close.

Okay, but if the book is neither endorsing federal debt nor government spending, where's the delusion? Isn't the total federal debt of roughly $36 trillion massive? Doesn't the previous number ignore just how much the U.S. Treasury owes, and isn't the combined number gargantuan? The answer to all three questions is yes.

At the same time, this book brings nuance to a subject that has long been accompanied with alarm. Without making a case for federal debt of any kind, *The Deficit Delusion* asks readers to think differently about what they've been hearing ad nauseum for decades.

Instead of just accepting the conventional wisdom about the meaning of the debt and the certain "crisis" that awaits, this book asks readers to consider a view that's well off the beaten path, as it were, a view that says the $36 trillion owed by the U.S. Treasury is, far from evidence of a looming debt crisis, the surest sign that there isn't one. And to be clear about what's just been written, the previous comment should in no way be construed as a veiled comment that Treasury debt is so large that it will never be paid, or that it will be defaulted on. Such a view isn't serious, and it won't be talked about here, except for in mocking tones.

At the same time, the notion that the debt is "unsustainable" will similarly be addressed in mocking tones. The surest sign the debt is *wholly sustainable* and will be easily paid back can paradoxically be found in the size of the debt that has the alarmists so up in arms.

And as indicated earlier, *The Deficit Delusion* also doesn't embrace the views expressed by left- or right-wing scolds that the debt can't be paid off due to its size, and so must be fixed with more revenue, taxes, or both. Such a view is hopelessly backward, as readers will see in this short book.

Readers may also expect the book to bring with it a supply-side happy talker tone about cutting taxes and stimulating economic activity that makes it possible for us to "grow" our way out of the deficits with more federal revenue. No, no such argument will be made here. The happy talkers will be routinely critiqued by a fellow supply-sider.

Which gets us to this book's true thrust: debt is a logical consequence of soaring revenue. Hence the long discussion of Uber and entrepreneurialism that begins this book. Uber's ascent from unknown to Unicorn to $157 billion noun, verb, and adjective explains something bigger than entrepreneurial achievement against all odds in the United States. In reality, it sets the stage for a discussion of the reason behind debt, and by extension why the scolds and happy talkers are wholly mangling basic understanding of debt with their delusions related to it.

CHAPTER ONE

They're All 30 Days from Bankruptcy, and Have No Debt

> *Businesses, like people, seldom if ever fail solely because of a lack of money. They fail because of a lack of ability, judgement, wisdom, ideas, organization, leadership. When those qualities are present, money is seldom a problem.*
> —Warren Brookes, *The Economy in Mind*, p. 172

It was the late 1990s and Nvidia was about to go out of business. Yes, you read that right. Nvidia was soon to vanish. Hard as it may be to believe considering the AI chipmaker's present status as the world's most valuable company, for the longest time Nvidia proved a very difficult company to keep alive.

In many ways, the then-and-now contrast isn't surprising. As the previous chapter stressed, true entrepreneurs are *extraordinary* for leading commerce in all new directions heretofore unimagined. *There's your $3 trillion valuation.* Had its business model been obvious, Nvidia wouldn't exist today. And it wouldn't exist simply because $3 trillion ideas don't lack for takers, or for feverish competition. If anyone of note had thought Nvidia's business plan had any reasonable chance of success, the minnow that became a giant would have been put out of business by much larger, better-funded competitors, or purchased by them.

Looked at through the prism of Vinod Khosla's enchantment with the impossible, Nvidia plainly achieved something like that. See the $3 trillion valuation again, and think about entrepreneurs in the 1990s trying to invent a future that would involve machines not just doing for us, but thinking for us. The internet was seen as wildly advanced back in the 1990s, so imagine how far-fetched AI would have seemed.

The sign put up at Nvidia's headquarters amid its major struggles to stay alive read: "Our company is thirty days from going out of business." It remains Nvidia's unofficial corporate motto.[1]

The problem was that its chips kept failing. As Ben Cohen explained it in the *Wall Street Journal*, Nvidia's "first chip was a flop. Its second one was doomed to fail." Think about this while remembering Uber and the $12 million it received in return for 20 percent of the company. Money for start-ups is tight, by definition. What's expected to fail isn't handed too much money to burn.

Applied to Nvidia, two failed chips put it in a precarious position. As the Warren Brookes quote that begins this chapter relates, companies don't run out of money; rather, they run out of investor confidence, or trust. And since most start-ups go belly-up as it is, one with two failed chips early on faced the inevitable cash crunch that most do.

What do you, the reader, speculate as the source of Nvidia's funding? Equity or debt? Quoting baseball great Bryce Harper, "clown question." What's expected to die isn't financed with debt. There aren't enough zeros for the interest rate necessary to properly match the risk associated with a start-up like Nvidia. It was equity finance, period. And the buyers of the equity plainly had little optimism that the company founded in a Denny's restaurant would make it. How we know this to be true can be found in the fact that there are no Nvidia *trillionaires* roaming the earth.

Regarding the situation Nvidia was in, Cohen adds that founder Jensen Huang knew the clock was ticking toward his company's extinction. The crisis for the Nvidia was "existential," hence the sign about thirty days to failure.[2]

Luckily for Huang, he'd made a good impression on Sega executive Shoichiro Irimajiri, and Irimajiri went to bat for Nvidia inside the video game giant. Sega invested $5 million in Nvidia, which was enough to keep it alive for another six months. To say that the rest is history is to suggest that it was smooth sailing after the investment. No, six months to live is the opposite of eternity when no one wants your equity. Still, Nvidia was at least saved thanks to Irimajiri convincing his boss at Sega to purchase $5 million worth of the then-foundering company.

Except that there's more. Sega eventually sold its stake at a 200 percent profit. Huge, right? If only all investments generated such returns. Sega turned $5 million into $15 million, but its massive return is yet another reminder of why Nvidia in the old days was solely funded with exchanges of equity for cash. And the answer is that even the executives at Sega weren't that sure about Nvidia's future. Had they been, it's no reach to say that the Sega of 2024 would have a $1 trillion+ grand slam of all grand slams on its books.

Still, Nvidia made it. And the world is a better place for its achievements. While this will be discussed more later in the book, it's useful to observe now about machines that they don't replace human action and thought as much as they amplify human skills. Call AI wildly compassionate. Alas, we're getting ahead of ourselves.

For now, it's important to think of Nvidia's near-death experiences considering a June 19, 2024, *Washington Post* headline about the U.S. national debt. It read like this: "National debt will hit $50.7 trillion by 2034, federal budget agency projects." The federal agency that reported what was roundly deemed bad news was the Congressional Budget Office (CBO).

If you the reader imagine that the news about the United States' allegedly dire debt situation made the front page of the *Post*, you would be incorrect. Which really isn't surprising. To see why, just Google "National Debt" and "Crisis." Paraphrasing the great satirist Christopher Buckley, if you do so your computer will explode.

So common is the notion of "national debt" and "crisis," so often is it bruited in the media by pundits, economists, and politicians, that it's no longer even front-page news. This is very telling, and as such will be addressed on a variety of levels throughout this book. For now, it will just be said that what's broadly accepted as a fait accompli (debt crisis) no longer rates front-page news. Which again says something, but it's best to inch toward what it says as a way of trying to elicit from readers an entirely different way of looking at debt.

For now, it's hardly novel to report the commentary that came with the CBO report. In the article mentioned, Maya MacGuineas (president of the nonpartisan Committee for a Responsible Federal Budget) was quoted as saying that "The risks we run from this growing mountain of debt run the gamut from slower economic growth to lower incomes, an inability to respond to emergencies and a weaker role in the world."[3] MacGuineas is a "go-to" voice on the matter of debt, and generally says the same thing over and over again. Every aspect of MacGuineas's statement will eventually be addressed in this book, but for now it's useful as a way of conveying just how anxious the national debt makes those who have a made a career out of following it.

That's what's so odd about the national debt discussion. Or maybe not. Just as bureaucracies are forever in search of a purpose, so by extension are pundits and activists like MacGuineas. Her organization exists to promote what she imagines is a "responsible" federal budget, which means it helps MacGuineas for the perception of federal budgeting to always be irresponsible. In which case the budget is always a problem to MacGuineas, and always has been a problem to economists, pundits, politicians, activists—you name it. Call the national debt the one policy area that left and right agree on. To be clear, they don't agree about solutions to what they naively deem the problem, but they do agree there is a problem. And it's the debt.

On the day that the aforementioned CBO report dropped, Andrew Wilford published a piece at RealClearMarkets that opened with: "The federal government faces a national debt crisis like never before in its history." Wilford is a policy analyst at the National Taxpayers Union Foundation, which is a right-leaning entity focused on government spending and taxes. Wilford followed his rather alarmist lede with "Most economists from across the political spectrum agree that the deficit is out of control and leading the country on the road to disaster."[4] Wilford doesn't lack for certitude, does he?

Notable about Wilford's piece is that he was rebutting *New York Times* columnist, Princeton economics professor, and right-wing bête noire commentator Paul Krugman. The view here, and throughout this book, is that Wilford didn't just overdo it with his commentary pregnant with "crisis" and "disaster" related to the debt, but that he's actually mistaking what the crisis is to begin with. It's assuredly not the debt, and that should not be construed as evidence of your author agreeing with Krugman.

While Krugman is of the view that deficits and debt don't matter, he's utterly confused about why they don't matter, and why size of the debt is the surest sign of a lack of a crisis. Basically, Wilford and Krugman are incorrect, but not for reasons they've deduced.

At the same time there's a kernel of truth within Krugman's view that the debt doesn't matter, as there is truth from Wilford that "most economists" believe the national debt foretells disaster. They do. Such a view is hardly partisan. It's not an exaggeration to say that of those who follow the federal budget, they all think a crisis looms.

Wilford is a Republican and believes as he does about the debt, while MacGuineas is an Independent. Ryan Bourne is the R. Evan Scharf Chair for the Public Understanding of Economics at the libertarian Cato Institute, but on the question of "how will the debt be defused," Bourne concludes that it's a "challenge worth obsessing about."[5] *Washington Post* economics columnist Catherine Rampell plainly leans left, or realistically, Democrat, but believes that "Our borrowing might finally come back to bite us," that a "fiscal reckoning could now be approaching,"[6] and all sorts of other theoretically scary stuff. Manhattan Institute senior fellow Jessica Riedl plainly leans right, or conservative, but she's even more alarmed than Rampell is. Interviewed by the *Washington Post* about the national debt in 2023, Riedl indicated that "The federal government is sitting on a ticking time bomb."

All of which hopefully further confirms for readers what's true, that the national debt is a bipartisan worry. Left and right are up in arms about it, yet the debt continues to grow. In 1980, total national debt was $900 billion,[7] yet as was previously mentioned, the debt today is $36 trillion on the way to $50.7 trillion, and on and on and on. Why, if "most economists" think the debt is so bad, and such a weight on future economic growth and income, does the debt keep going up? No doubt some are seeking an answer to the question, but the more realistic answer is that most reading this book *know* the answer, or *think* they do.

Some are surely murmuring to themselves that debt springs from too much spending, others surely mimic the Keynesian–Krugman line that it's the Republicans' fault, others think it's surely the fault of free-spending Democrats, while supply-side happy talkers imagine it's a function of taxes being too high and the incentive to work too low, such that revenues aren't high enough to pay off all the debt. Yes, the same old stuff. The arguments never change. And they certainly didn't change in response to the latest projections of debt of the $50 trillion variety.

The good news is that those same arguments will not be made in this book. And that's not because your author chooses to be contrarian, but instead because the arguments are weak. And silly. And realistically non sequiturs.

As mentioned in the introduction, *The Deficit Delusion* asks readers to think differently about the national debt. It's most definitely easy to embrace conventional wisdom, which will never get you in trouble, but the embrace of the conventional over the decades by "most economists" has hardly brought down the national debt, assuming that doing so is the answer to what so many deem a crisis. Therefore, it's not just useful to look at government spending and the national debt differently, it's arguably *essential*. The warring ideologies have quite simply gotten us nowhere on the matter of spending and the debt, unless persistent predictions of doom going back decades represent progress. Sorry, but "crying wolf" repeatedly hardly sounds like progress, particularly when the debt cried about by the wolves has soared.

All of which requires a pivot back to Uber, and Nvidia after Uber. Readers who remember the introduction, and who internalized the trajectory of Uber from unknown to Unicorn to $157 billion noun, verb, and adjective could be excused for wondering why all the worry about the national debt in the first place. They might even find themselves thinking that the debt and deficit hawks across the ideological spectrum have it all backward.

Uber never had debt when it was largely an unknown staring at a future that would most likely be defined by bankruptcy, and a quick bankruptcy at that. I will repeat it repeatedly, no one lends to businesses expected to go bankrupt simply because no one lends with an eye on getting nothing in return for a substantial something. In other words, the "predatory lending" that excited members of the economic, political, and pundit classes back in 2008 was a total laugh.

It's also a laugh in 2024 when economists, politicians, and pundits claim the United States is bankrupt. (About bankruptcy, if your computer didn't explode when you googled "debt" and "crisis," try "U.S." and "bankrupt" to finish the job.) How could an entity that will apparently soon have over $50 trillion in debts be bankrupt? How indeed.

Still, we're talking about Uber. Unable to borrow back in 2011, in 2025 the company, as previously mentioned, has over $11 billion in debts. What a change. As for Nvidia, while it couldn't borrow a dollar back in the 1990s, it too can now claim over $11 billion worth of debt on its books. No surprise there.

For a company that can presently claim a market cap greater than $3 trillion, $11 billion is quite literally a rounding error. Better yet, it's debt! Uber and Nvidia formerly had to give away so much equity for so little, and they had to because companies never run out of money; rather, they run out of investor trust. Equity financing of old was a market signal of low investor trust in their respective futures.

Just the same, the debt signals enormous investor trust in their respective futures. This can be seen in their enormous valuations. Which requires a quick revisit with venture capitalist Peter Thiel. As he put it in *Zero to One*, "Simply stated, the value of a business today is the sum of all the money it will make in the future." Applying Thiel's valuation approach to Uber and Nvidia, readers can then see just how tiny each company's debt is relative to what they're expected to make in the future. To be clear, the debt on the books of Uber and Nvidia is a market signal of enormous economic health. Both are expected to make lots of money, and by extension both have investors lined up to loan them money.

Is the money "easy"? No, because there's no such thing. Evidence that there's no such thing can be found in the total lack of debt for Uber and Nvidia back in their early stages. So "tight" was money for Uber and Nvidia back in the 1990s and 2011 that no interest rate was high enough to lend to them. Once again, equity finance was their only option. Money is relatively "easy" for both today simply because each company's growth and expected growth has been nothing short of miraculous. Put another way, Uber and Nvidia had to endure brutally hard years so that money could be relatively "easy." The debt is yet again a sign of health.

Just the same, the fact that the debt on Uber and Nvidia's books signals immense health for each raises questions about the federal government, and, yes, its debt. Writing about the debt and the CBO report previously discussed in this chapter, an editorial on the left-leaning *Washington Post*'s editorial page indicated that it "is not a cause for celebration." Actually, "Nearly every part of this latest CBO report is alarming," at least according to the editorial.[8]

Notable here is that the right-leaning editorial page at the *Wall Street Journal* was hardly optimistic about the same report. Members of the editorial board there indicated that the "CBO's budget forecasts are getting progressively uglier," and that failure to address all the presumed ugliness sets the stage for "either a monumental tax increase or a debt panic down the road."[9] On the left, and in a piece for the *Wall Street Journal* titled "The National Debt Crisis Is Coming," Brookings Institution senior fellow William Galston wrote that "Continuing on our current fiscal course will mean a gradual loss of America's financial independence followed by an abrupt economic decline."[10] And then longtime deficit wolf Jessica Riedl not surprisingly chimed in about the CBO report that "These are the ingredients of a debt crisis," that "such a dire outlook requires Washington's attention," and that "these escalating deficits are unsustainable, as the laws of economics and mathematics always eventually win."[11]

Hmmm. Something's not right. No doubt Riedl is right in a superficial sense that the "laws of economics and mathematics always eventually win," but who says they don't? As we've seen with Uber and Nvidia, the debt markets are very exacting markets. And they are because no one, nowhere parts with money blithely. Which is why Uber and Nvidia couldn't run up debt when their futures were expected to be brief and defined by bankruptcy. But once the two corporations became great, as it were, their ability to borrow naturally grew with the greatness.

Precisely because they're expected to make a lot of money in the future, Uber and Nvidia can borrow a lot now. Okay, but how is the

United States different? About the question, readers will be asked not to falsely construe it as a defense of government spending. The latter is the biggest economy- and progress-sapping tax of all. This viewpoint will be found throughout *The Deficit Delusion*.

At the same time, readers could be excused at this point for perhaps raising an eyebrow to the conventional wisdom about debt expressed by left and right in the United States. Sorry, but debt is rarely a signal of trouble ahead simply because debt is issued in the marketplace, and the marketplace and market prices are a look into the future. Looking into the future, the expectation is that the national debt will be quite a bit higher. Without once again excusing government spending for even a second, and similarly without blaming government spending as the cause of the debt, it will be said right here that contra all the alarm, projections of rising debt are hardly indicative of economic troubles ahead. To suggest otherwise, as the pundit class near unanimously does, implies not just market stupidity, but *ferocious* amounts of market stupidity.

Which requires a pause. How could someone who loathes government spending, but who doesn't blame debt on government spending, not see the government debt as the problem? Better yet, how could this individual see projections of future debt as a bullish signal while loathing government spending and government debt in parallel fashion? They're worthy questions, and they're worth thinking about before turning to the next chapter.

This book promised to make you think differently, or at least consider thinking differently from the same crisis-mongering, gloom and doom, crisis-is-ahead mode of thought that has always defined the debt discussion. So there you have it. Start asking the question: if government spending saps growth and progress, but government debt isn't the problem, what is the problem? Please keep reading.

CHAPTER TWO

Not Just Any Government Can Run Up Debt

There are croakers in every country, always boding its ruin. Such a one then lived in Philadelphia; a person of note, an elderly man, with a wise look and a very grave manner of speaking; his name was Samuel Mickle.... This man continued to live in this decaying place, and to declaim in the same strain, refusing for many years to buy a house there, because all was going to destruction; and at last I had the pleasure of seeing him give five times as much for one as he might have bought it for when he first began his croaking.[1]
—Benjamin Franklin

According to *Forbes*, Nike cofounder Phil Knight is worth $40 billion. Why is Knight so incredibly rich?

The seemingly obvious response brings us once again to Bryce Harper: it's a "clown question." Don't you get it? Knight is worth $40 billion because he created a global shoe and sports apparel brand. Basic stuff.

Except that this book disdains what's perceived as obvious simply because accepted wisdom frequently obscures greater, much more important truths. Phil Knight is not worth $40 billion because he cofounded Nike, rather, he's worth $40 billion because vanishingly few, including at times Knight himself, thought the company he cofounded had any chance of succeeding.

That banks wouldn't touch Knight and Blue Ribbon Sports (the name of Nike before it was Nike) is a blinding glimpse of what we've already seen. Banks lend to those who can pay them back, and the broad expectation of those who'd actually heard of Knight's company was that it would not survive—which made a loan a nonstarter.

And yet Nike did survive, which requires a brief digression in order to elicit different thinking from readers. Imagine for a second if the Fed had lowered borrowing rates to "zero" in 1970. As Knight explained it in his incomparably great 2016 memoir, *Shoe Dog*, "1970 was the summer of liquidity, and I had none."[2]

Okay, but what if the Fed went to "zero"? According to Ruchir Sharma, head of Rockefeller Capital Management's international business, the Fed can do this. As Sharma put it in his 2024 book *What Went Wrong With Capitalism*, "When the price of borrowing money is zero, the price of everything else goes bonkers."[3] Of course, the problem with Sharma's allusion is that it's utter nonsense.

Sharma's line from his much-commented-on book is that the Fed has the power to decree borrowing artificially cheap or costless, and has done just that from 1980 to the present. Except that it can do no such thing, and you the reader likely know why by now.

Simply put, the notion that the Fed can decree credit costless as imagined by Sharma (and sadly, much of the commentariat) is as divorced from reality as is the notion that lawmakers could decree a $100/hour minimum wage. About the latter, no doubt lawmakers could legislate the nosebleed wage, but providers of it would be few to nonexistent. Businesses generally aren't in the business of going out of business in order to pay wages they can't afford to pay.

What's missed is that those with title to money are no different. While the Fed can "hike" or "reduce" interest rates to whatever level the would-be central planners inside the central bank imagine is correct, the markets for money and credit will always sing their own tune. Readers have already happened upon the impressive fatuity of Sharma's thinking through the stories of Nvidia and Uber. While each came into existence when the Fed was "reducing" its Fed funds rate to low single digits on the way to "zero," there was no borrowing at "zero" for either start-up, nor was there borrowing for either at all. As I will repeat again and again, for start-ups in search of a loan there's no interest rate high enough to compensate the lender.

From there, let's just use common sense in addressing flamboyant foolishness that informs not just the Fed's actions, but the analysis of the Fed by pundits. Simply put, its biggest critics (Sharma is a critic) actually believe the Fed capable of decreeing credit costless. No, not at all.

Such a view implies that compound interest, one of the great "wonders of the world," is actually powerless relative to people with last names like Bernanke, Yellen, and Powell; that if central bankers decree the cost of borrowing zero, those with title to money throw the genius of compound interest and returns out the window in order to hand the money away for—yes—free. No, the view is not serious.

Back to reality, there's no such thing as cheap or "easy money" in capitalism. Money is always and everywhere rather expensive precisely because the cost of zero returns, low returns, or negative returns resulting from foolish lending is so great. Think of the genius of compounding interest yet again. Precisely because wealth put to work wisely compounds so brilliantly, there's no incentive nor any need to lend it for zero interest. Demand for "money" at rates much greater than zero is always there, and then as Nvidia and Uber remind us, so great is demand for money that the vast majority of entrepreneurs and businesses will offer up *equity* in return for it; as in they'll pay exponentially more for capital than any central planner at the Fed could ever hope to imagine.

Which hopefully explains the digression. To convince readers to think differently, it's essential to address the sources of faulty conventional thinking. Sharma's book about what allegedly went wrong with capitalism is popular precisely due to the conventional view that the Fed not only controls the amount of credit in the economy, but also its cost. Except that it doesn't, and never has.

Bringing it all back to Phil Knight and his "summer of liquidity" in 1970, it wouldn't have helped him one iota if the Federal Reserve had done in 1970 (reduced interest rates to zero) what Sharma and so many conventional thinkers suggest the Fed has done to varying degrees from 1980 to the present. Say it over and over again: There's not a rate high enough to compensate lenders for providing cash to entrepreneurs or businesses for whom an earnings future of any kind is uncertain.

That was Knight's problem, but it also explains his enormous net worth today. Knight was clear on the matter of liquidity that he "had none" in 1970. Perhaps more interestingly, but also not surprisingly, what followed the previous admission was Knight's recollection that "I spent most of every day thinking about liquidity, talking about liquidity, looking to the heavens and pleading for liquidity. My kingdom for liquidity."[4]

That lenders weren't beating down the door to Knight's headquarters (they were located above a seedy bar in Portland, Oregon) is almost a waste of words. Worse for Knight is that it wasn't just the lending window that was shut to him. So was the equity finance option. Knight was literally praying for liquidity, and would have gladly exchanged shares in his nascent shoe company in return for liquidity, but there were no takers. Which again explains Knight's wealth today. He owned and owns much more Nike equity in the present simply because demand for it in the past was nearly nonexistent. Entrepreneurial success is yet again a miracle, or rooted in the impossible, and the wealth that the highly rare successes eventually amass is a reflection of just how low their odds of success are seen to be.

Knight is a useful way to begin this chapter as a way of conveying just how rare, and arguably *luxurious* debt is. The ability to run up debt implies a view in the marketplace that the individual or corporation in question has a future. Knight was seen as lacking one, hence his daily prayers for liquidity.

Which brings us to Alexander Hamilton, the first U.S. Treasury secretary. Long before taking the oath of office, Hamilton had made plain his views that the United States required taxing power and the debt that the latter would enable as a way of establishing credit in the marketplace. In an April 1781 letter written to Philadelphia banker and fellow founding father Robert Morris, Hamilton asserted that "a national debt, if not excessive, will be to us a national blessing."[5] Which requires a pause.

About the previous paragraph, make no mistake about the mention of Hamilton, taxes, debt, and subsequent credit: it is not an endorsement of taxes (whether on tariffs or income), government spending, or government borrowing. It will be discussed throughout the book, but government spending is yet again a huge economy- and freedom-sapping tax. That is so because governments must extract precious wealth from the source of production and wealth creation (the private sector) in order to decree where precious wealth goes. It's a short way of saying that government spending amounts to the centralized allocation of precious resources. Yes, central planning. The latter never works.

At the same time, it should be said that Hamilton was right. The United States lacked credit and the ability to borrow because it didn't have much of a history of tax collection, tax collection in the present, or the expectation of tax-revenue collection in the future. It's worth adding that more than a few people, including people living in what became the United States, didn't think the U.S. had a future. See the

Ben Franklin quote that begins this chapter. And readers all know by now how difficult borrowing is when the future is uncertain, or worse, seen as bleak.

In 1781, Hamilton was looking into the future. Once the would-be country would become the *United States*, it would need proof of its ability to tax in order to borrow. About the borrowing, readers can agree or disagree about the good or bad of it, but what they can't disagree with is the validity of Hamilton's contention that in order to issue debt, what would become the U.S. Treasury would have to showcase for the markets an ability not just to collect taxes, but collect progressively more taxes in the future.

Again, think back to the point made just four paragraphs ago: the existence or issuance of debt implies a view in the marketplace that the individual or corporation in question has a future. This is so true, and it cannot be stressed enough that governments are no different. Money that actually exchanges for real wealth (the only kind of money to borrow) is far too precious to be loaned out carelessly. The genius of compound interest yet again underscores this simple truth. And since good, credible money is precious, those interested in borrowing must provide potential lenders (a.k.a. "the markets") with powerful evidence that they have a future that will enable the payback of monies borrowed.

So, while one of the principal Founding Fathers in Hamilton believed it necessary that the United States have taxing power in order to borrow money and pay monies back to establish credit in the marketplace, not everyone agreed with him. Most notably, Thomas Jefferson didn't agree.

Jefferson felt government debt amounted to a form of "slavery" for taxpayers, and that the issuance of it and marketing of it would create opportunities for the Wall Street "moneyed interests" that he disdained. In a preview of the twentieth- and twenty-first-century politicians who would romanticize jobs in factories and mills, Jefferson's romance was with the soil. In the words of Duke University professor Richard Salsman from his 2017 book *The Political Economy of Public Debt*, "As a physiocrat," Jefferson believed "only agrarian life preserves virtue." In Jefferson's own words, "those who labor in the Earth are the chosen people of God."[6] Jefferson was the anti-Hamilton, or Hamilton the anti-Jefferson.

At the same time, Jefferson recognized that the ability to borrow was a function of an ability to take in revenue. Which means Jefferson was worlds ahead of modern thinkers who literally believe the cost of credit and its amount is planned by central banks. It's safe to say the Founding Father would have a lot of fun with the conceit of those prone to believing that interest rates are whatever central bankers decide they should be. Let's call Jefferson a pessimistic realist on the matter of a national debt.

While he didn't want the U.S. Treasury to issue debt for reasons already explained, Jefferson felt it necessary that the U.S. Treasury possess the *ability* to borrow. It was a national security issue for Jefferson. The United States needed to be able to borrow in an emergency, which on its own may raise eyebrows among some readers. Goodness, emergencies are crucial sustenance for politicians. No reach there. Still, in a 1788 letter, Jefferson conceded the importance of the U.S. Treasury having credit. He wrote that "Though much an enemy to the system of borrowing . . . I feel strongly the necessity of preserving the power to borrow."[7]

And so the United States began to tax and borrow. The formerly bankrupt country that couldn't borrow would reveal through rising tax revenues an ability to do just that. In the words of Salsman, the aim was to "show the world the United States *could* and *would* pay its debts," which "conveyed strength and elicited the confidence of creditors."[8] Which on its face is interesting. Hamilton saw debt as a signal of strength, as evidence of the ability of the United States to borrow and pay back monies owed. Yet as we've seen throughout this book, debt is often viewed by economists and pundits across the spectrum as a scary signal of future doom. Which is backward.

About this, it will be said once again that government spending is a horrid freedom- and economy-sapping tax. What enables the centralized and politicized allocation of previous resources is by its very description inimical to freedom and economic growth. But in isolation, is the debt enabling such spending a sign of trouble ahead of the "crisis" variety? The very notion suggests impressive stupidity in the marketplace that rarely reveals itself in debt markets for companies, and as readers will see in the next chapter, for individuals. How are governments any different?

Even if some do actually lend out money carelessly, we see through the past, present, and future borrowing of the United States that it's capable of borrowing enormous amounts of money. To suggest that lending to the United States is the stuff of easy, or "dumb" money, suggests foolish money circulates the world on an enormous scale. In other words, it suggests what is logically, and powerfully false. And it can be found yet again in the debt trajectory of the United States. Per Hamilton, the United States had to prove it had taxing power now and in the future in order to borrow. It would once again borrow and pay monies back to establish credit in a marketplace full of skeptics.

Which requires a return to the present. As has been discussed throughout this book, the CBO projects national debt of $50.7 trillion in 2034. And according to the deepest of deep thinkers on the left and right, the latter foretells a massive crisis. It also supposedly signals bankruptcy.

To see what is meant by all the pessimism surrounding the debt, just look at the opinion piece titles by Cato Institute senior fellow Doug Bandow in recent years to get a flavor of what passes and has passed for accepted wisdom with regard to the national debt: "Republicans Accelerate America's Rush Toward Bankruptcy," "As U.S. Goes

Bankrupt, How Many Foreign Crises Can It Afford?," "Republicans Glory In Financial Bankruptcy," and to show that Bandow isn't solely hard on Republicans, let's throw in "Headed for Insolvency: Biden Administration Increases U.S. Obligations Worldwide." About Bandow, the previous titles are just a sampling of decades' worth of columns from him about a bankrupt, or going-bankrupt United States. And Bandow is not alone. This is how self-proclaimed budget or deficit hawks view the United States' deficit or debt situation.

Which hopefully has readers more than a bit skeptical by now. Think Uber and Nvidia yet again. But also think what Alexander Hamilton was trying to make happen at the founding of the United States. *Debt was the goal.* It signaled rising prosperity for the United States not because of the borrowing, but because the borrowing represented rising prosperity within the United States, rising tax revenues as a consequence of that prosperity, and an ability to borrow as a result of rising tax revenues.

How, if the United States is bankrupt, can it borrow so much now, and according to the CBO, well into the future? Hopefully the answer to this question is a little bit clearer at this point. The answer is that—love or hate government borrowing—the United States is *not* bankrupt. Quite the opposite. Since exceedingly few throw away money or disdain potential returns, there's no way the United States could be borrowing trillions a year now and into the future if it were bankrupt. Sorry, but there's not nearly enough dumb money in the world to fund all of the United States' borrowing.

It's a long, or perhaps short, way of saying that per Nvidia and Uber, but also per Alexander Hamilton, the United States can borrow in enormous amounts now because it takes in tax revenue in enormous amounts, but much more important, its borrowing in enormous amounts will continue well into the future because lenders expect tax collections for the U.S. Treasury to grow, and grow, and grow.

Jessica Riedl, William Galston, Maya MacGuineas among many, many others see a "debt crisis" in the United States' future, but the borrowing by the United States signals that investors with actual skin in the game see quite the opposite. In other words, and without defending the soaring debt of the United States for even a second, its existence is a sign that the United States' future is blindingly bright. Repeat it over and over again that the U.S. Treasury can borrow enormous amounts of money cheaply because it takes in a lot of money in taxes now and is expected to take in a lot more in the future. There's the debt. The debt is yet again a consequence of soaring revenues now, and the expectation of exponentially more revenues in the future.

Please keep the above truths running through your head as the left-leaning Galston asserts that "Politicians need to recognize the urgency of cutting benefits or raising revenue."[9] And it's not just Galston who thinks more tax revenues are the solution to the alleged deficit or debt "problem." Mentioned in the last chapter was Cato economist Ryan Bourne, a libertarian. Bourne asserts that in order to "avoid ever-escalating debt (which nobody thinks is sustainable), we are going to have to see substantive spending cuts or tax revenue rises."[10] The irony of Bourne's alarmism is that he claims "nobody" thinks the borrowing is sustainable, which is an employee of a market-oriented think tank's way of saying markets are really stupid. But that's a digression. The more important point is that the libertarian in Bourne, who has a wildly different view of government and its proper role and size than does Galston, agrees with Galston about the solution for the alleged debt problem.

Moving back to the left and Rampell, so concerned about the debt is she that her aim is to further empower the IRS. In her words at the *Washington Post*, "Every dollar available for auditing taxpayers generates many times that amount for government coffers."[11] Oh boy, there those "liberal lovers" of big government go again.... Well, not so fast.

Writing in the *Washington Post* herself, archconservative Manhattan Institute budget expert Jessica Riedl wrote that shrinking funding for the IRS "is not a conservative move." As she sees it, "we need this revenue" from an empowered IRS, and that a failure to more aggressively fund the IRS "will ultimately drive up deficits and raise middle class taxes."

Why all these examples? They're employed to sear into the minds of readers that fear of debt and deficits is bipartisan, or let's call it multipartisan. And the solution from the warring ideologies is invariably the same: more tax revenues on the left, less spending and more taxes on the right (though arguments for reduced spending implicitly say that government revenues aren't sufficient). Both arguments are wrongheaded and naive. Think yet again about Uber and Nividia's path to debt, along with the path to debt sketched by Alexander Hamilton. What enables more debt is more revenue.

This is basic, basic stuff, yet it's never said. What should be said is that national debt is a direct consequence of way too much tax revenue now, and the expectation of much more tax revenue in the future. In other words, the logical path to reduced debt is greatly reduced federal revenue. Except that this point isn't being made. Instead, the deficit scolds say a slight variation of the same thing over and over again.

And then there are the supply-siders. Too happy to scold, they write endlessly about ways to maximize government revenues. They claim the latter is about reducing the deficits and debt, but in reality it's their unwitting way of directing more money to Congress so that it can centrally plan the allocation of precious resources. Which means supply-siders, rather than making the crucial removal of governmental barriers to production their goal, have instead made themselves most known for pursuing the tax rate at which the greatest amount of government revenue will be raised. To quote prominent supply-sider Donald Luskin from a 2005 opinion piece written at *National Review*

Online, "I love the smell of tax revenues in the morning. It smells like victory."[12]

For Luskin's clever riff on a line from the classic film *Apocalypse Now*, credit will be given. Luskin is very smart, and creative too. And while rising tax revenues aren't victory, they at least signal for readers the problem: the federal government collects way too much in taxes, hence all the federal debt. The debt is an effect of too much tax collection. So, while the debt is a sign of abundant U.S. prosperity, it's also a signal that government has arrogated for its own redistribution far too much of the earnings of the world's most prosperous people.

CHAPTER THREE

Let's Be Serious: Deficits Are NOT An Effect of Too Much Spending

> *Ask any rich man of common prudence, to which of the two sorts of people he has lent the greater part of his stock, to those who, he thinks, will employ it profitably, or those who will spend it idly, and he will laugh at you for proposing the question.*
> —Adam Smith, *The Wealth of Nations*, p. 381

Love or hate Donald Trump, some historians will ultimately observe that he was way ahead of his time. Rest assured, the previous sentence is not political.

What makes Trump ahead of his time is that he's on his *third* career. He started in real estate development, pivoted very successfully to television in 2004, then in 2015 a rather famous ride down an escalator signaled his move into politics.

In the future, lifetimes defined by a variety of careers will be the norm. The source of this exciting development will be the very division of labor between people, machines, and thinking machines around the world that needlessly has so many so worried about their ability to find work in the future. The worry is well overdone.

What replaces aspects of what we do (whether by people in another country or machines) doesn't put us out of work as much as it amplifies our talents. When we can divide up tasks with others, or leave tasks to others (including machines) altogether, our odds of specializing on the job soar. And when we can do what we're really good at, work is no longer work. It's joy.

The explosion of the global labor division will unearth all sorts of jobs heretofore unimagined, but that mirror our unique skills and intelligence in ways they don't now, and most certainly didn't in the past. The result will be that talented people more and more jump from successful career to successful career as a path to self-fulfillment that wasn't available for generations past.

Yet this chapter is not about work, nor is this book about work, except through indirect commentary. The focus here as readers know is debt, and this chapter in particular will address the good or bad of budget deficits and country debt. This is important simply because some may have gotten the impression—despite numerous pauses so far in which government spending was disdained—that the book you're reading is meant to praise government spending, country debt, or both. No. Quite the opposite.

Government debt signals the extraction of precious resources from the private economy (where all production takes place, by definition), and the politicized redistribution of the wealth extracted. The impact is bad for the vast majority of us. And that's true regardless of the politicians doing the borrowing and redistributing. Government spending is once again a freedom- and economy-sapping tax, as is government borrowing.

Unlike most of the books written by economists, politicians and pundits, this book rejects the popular notion that the deficits and debt are a consequence of too little government revenue, too much government spending, or both. No, the deficits and debt are plainly a consequence of the U.S. Treasury collecting way too much in taxes now, and much worse, the expectation that Treasury will collect quite a bit more in tax revenues in the future. We have $36 trillion in debt (and counting) because Americans are prodigious creators of wealth that Treasury owns a piece of.

This debt in no way boosts our prosperity as the Paul Krugmans of the world believe, but it most certainly is a consequence of prosperity. And just as the Krugmans of the world have the implications of our debt backward, so do the deficit scolds on the left and right (think Bourne, Rampell, Riedl, MacGuineas, Bandow, etc.) have it backward when they promise month after month, year after year, and decade after decade that a "debt crisis" is coming. Oh please.

To see the fatuity of both sides about debt, Russia rates a brief detour. The Bank of Russia estimates that total debt for the country (or Federation) amounts to roughly $300 billion. Yes, you read that right, *billion*. That's it. $300 billion is a rounding error for the United States. So small at this point that it's hard to reasonably compare Russian Federation debt to the United States' of something north of $36 trillion—and higher every single year. $300 billion?

What's the story here? Is Vladimir Putin a closet classical economic thinker, or a Milton Friedman–style economic thinker who views government spending and borrowing as a cruel tax on freedom and prosperity? Clown question! Of course not.

In truth, and this is no insight, Russia has very little debt simply because investors don't trust its economic future. Basic stuff. Extremely basic.

Please think about how basic this while considering all the quotes you've read so far (and will read) from economic types claiming a "debt crisis" looms for the United States. About this alleged debt crisis that the scolds have been promising all of my life, and throughout the lives of every reader (maybe you're one of those scolds?), can it be concluded in parallel fashion that Russia has a much brighter, crisis-free future precisely because its total debt is a microscopic fraction of ours? You guessed it, another clown question.

Russia's tiny debt situation (relative to ours) is a market signal that its future is once again viewed rather negatively by investors with actual skin in the game. At the same time, U.S. debt signals investors with real money on the line view our future as much, much brighter, and much less crisis-ridden than Russia's. In other words, the information-pregnant markets don't share the pessimism of the scolds who populate the various ideologies.

The United States leads other countries in debt, and no one else is anywhere close. Certainly not poor old Russia. But before you feel too sad for Russia, it could be much worse. Think Haiti. It can claim total debt of *$6.72 billion*. Again, the debt isn't something to celebrate on its own, but the meaning of debt is something to celebrate. High national debt is a signal of national prosperity without it doing anything to boost national prosperity. The debt is an effect. See Uber and Nvidia again.

Which requires a pivot back to Donald Trump and his days as a real estate developer. The time was the late 1980s, and Trump was in pursuit of a loan that he would use to revitalize the Ambassador Hotel in Los Angeles. Yes, *that* Ambassador, where Robert F. Kennedy was tragically assassinated on June 6, 1968.

Subsequent to the tragedy, the hotel and the location around it had taken a dive. Which is where Trump enters the picture. A lover of name brands, he saw potential in reviving what was famous for reasons good and bad, but that also formerly connoted luxury.

With these thoughts in mind, Trump visited Los Angeles–based Security Pacific National Bank (then the largest U.S. bank) to meet with its new CEO, Robert Smith. Describing Trump in his own business memoirs, *Dead Bank Walking*, Smith recalled that when he first met him that Trump "had already been heralded as a genius and seemed to be at the leading edge of everything." Smith added that Trump "had a Clintonesque aura around him, the effervescent divinity of a studied deal-maker, and a categorical ability to communicate and inspire the belief of others in his personal vision. He no doubt could have been an evangelist." Keep in mind that Smith published his book in 1995. He plainly saw something, and that too is not a political statement.

Impressed as Smith was by how Trump carried himself, banks were not and are not in the business of lending to those who need the money. Get it? Banks make loans that they fully expect to be paid back.

In Trump's case, he asked for a $50 million loan as the starting point of his revitalization plan. While you consider his request, try to remove politics from it regardless of which way you lean. Instead, think of the Trump who walked in to see Smith. While people were surprised he ran for president in 2016, in the late eighties and nineties his name was regularly bruited as a possible presidential choice. He was thought to have a Midas touch. Yet Smith for the most part turned him down. "For the most part" will be gotten to just ahead, but for now it should be said that turning down such a famous name was on its own quite something.

Yet Smith had his reasons, and they are reasons that readers will surely understand much better now. As Smith explained it, "As a lender, no matter how glamorous the person on the other side of the table is, *you look to the borrower to have both primary and alternate sources of repayment.*" The emphasis? Your author. At this point we can translate the meaning of Smith's words, though they likely require no translation. What Smith conveyed nearly thirty years ago is that money is ruthless—loaned money in particular. It's got to be paid back, and since it must be, the borrower must be able to present credible evidence of income (think revenues) to the lender. The problem was that Trump could not.

Smith adds that "while Trump presented a financial statement with many million dollars of net worth, the ability of him to bail even this one project out was limited—because it was leveraged on an illiquid base of questionable value." To get a loan you must have income to pay off the loan. That's why Uber, Nvidia, a young United States, and even a future president at times had the proverbial loan window closed to them.

Back to "for the most part," it seems Trump's celebrity ultimately proved too much for some of Smith's colleagues at Security Pacific. And they approved a loan to him of $10 million for a "study on the feasibility of restoring the Ambassador Hotel." Trump didn't repay the loan amid a difficult property market in the early 1990s that proved very damaging to his own finances. The loan was eventually written off.[1]

Trump is a useful discussion as a reminder yet again of what lenders are looking for when they make loans. They must see a future defined by revenue inflows, or highly liquid assets necessary to pay off loans that income perhaps will not. Trump had neither in the late eighties, thus Smith's rejection of a $50 million request.

Yet the story continues, it's about Trump, and it continues in a way that gets us to our ongoing discussion of why government spending and debt are growth deterrents despite the paradoxical truth that both represent prosperity. From October 2023 to January 2024, Trump was on trial (*Trump v. New York*) for civil fraud charges related to exaggerating the worth of his various property holdings to attain more in the way of loans and at better terms (interest rate).

On the face of it, what an odd lawsuit! And you don't have to be a Trump supporter to observe that. Think back to Smith's recollections to see why. It's worth repeating his observation that "As a lender, no matter how glamorous the person on the other side of the table is, you look to the buyer to have both primary and alternate sources of repayment." In other words, loaned money is once again ruthless. As the Adam Smith quote that begins this chapter reminds us, no one parts ways with money easily. And in particular they don't when the borrower seeks large amounts as Trump long has.

Which is just a way of saying that Trump's exaggeration of his net worth to banks and other financial institutions was a statement of the obvious, but also immaterial. About the exaggeration, or "deception" by Trump and others close to him, that's the nature of real estate or realistically any other kind of investment. *Of course* the owner sees qualities in it that others perhaps don't. If not, he or she wouldn't be an owner.

Yet to say Trump deceived banks and financial institutions implies that markets aren't just dumb, but impressively so. It's also to pretend that Trump's massive, braggy reputation didn't precede him before he met with financial institutions to allegedly "deceive" them. Please. No chance. Precisely because Trump was Trump, and had a long track record of talking up his assets, his net worth, his various romantic conquests, and surely other things, it's a safe bet that no one was fooled.

Which brings us back to *Washington Post* columnist Catherine Rampell, someone who's been quoted here and there already. Rampell is a national debt or deficit hawk, and also a big-time Trump critic. Writing about the civil lawsuit in its aftermath, Rampell lamented that "while bank executives might have turned a blind eye to Trump's fraud does not necessarily mean there were no victims. Giving Trump financial products he should not have qualified for ultimately reduced resources available for other, honest borrowers."[2] What a sentiment! It's quite the sentiment because it carries meaning well beyond Trump and his exaggerations that allegedly won him more and better loan terms.

In Rampell's critique of Trump's dealings with banks, Rampell unwittingly happened on the problem with government spending or borrowing. It doesn't just happen. Using Rampell's exact words, government spending can only happen insofar as there are "reduced resources available for other" honest workers, businesses, and entrepreneurs. Unless Rampell thinks the government extracts resources from another planet, then it's logically true that the good, bad, or realistically horrid of government spending is a certain consequence of others going without.

Yet there's more, and it can be found in Rampell's along with Jessica Riedl's commentary from the previous chapter about how important it is for the IRS to have quite a bit more funding so that it can extract more tax revenues from the private sector. They claim these extra revenues are necessary to bring down the national debt. Of course, in calling for a bigger, more effective IRS, Rampell is at least alluding to the reality that governments can only spend insofar as those who pay taxes have less to spend. Well, yes. And as readers know, the ability for government to borrow grows in relation to the revenue it takes in. And this, per Rampell's very own expressed logic, means "reduced resources available for other, honest borrowers."

Government not only extracts with taxes, but also through borrowing. And its ability to borrow is a function of what it takes in via taxes. Either way, the losers are those who must go without as the size of government grows. It's a long way of saying that while Rampell's logic is sound in the sense that two people, or two businesses, or two governments can't borrow the same dollars, that same logic contradicts Rampell's assertion, along with those of Bourne, Galston, Riedl, MacGuineas and other deficit/debt hawks that the solution to debt is more tax revenue. *No.*

The revenues are what enable the debt, period. If Donald Trump had been able to prove credible income to Security Pacific in the late eighties, his loan would have been approved. But since he could not, it wasn't. The U.S. Treasury can borrow in enormous amounts because its revenue intake is highly credible, and growing more credible all the time. Let's not enhance its borrowing credibility with more tax revenue!

The problem, of course, is that these basic truths are fully absent from the present debt discussion. The focus is always on too little revenue, too much spending, or too little tax revenue because taxes are too high, but never on the actual problem of too much spending and too much borrowing directly born of way too much government revenue now and the expectation of even greater amounts in the future.

To provide more examples of how contradictory the discussion has become, consider a post by libertarian economist Dan Mitchell in the aftermath of the oft-mentioned (in this book) CBO report. On his "International Liberty" blog, Mitchell penned a write-up titled "The Looming Fiscal Crisis" that quoted substantially from a *Washington Times* column by another libertarian economist Richard Rahn and that bore the title "Is there any way out of the global debt crisis?" In Rahn's piece he claimed that "The correct policy solution is to cut government spending so that the debt-to-GDP ratio is falling at a meaningful rate," to which Mitchell responded "Amen. The United States needs a spending cap," and that "spending is the problem" while "debt is a symptom of the problem."[3] But for the regularly ignored truth that the debt is a logical symptom of too much revenue. If it were an effect of too much spending, then every government would have loads of debt. Except that markets for money are brutal. Only governments known to take in a lot of revenue in the present and expected to take in much more in the future can borrow. The main thing is that Mitchell and Rahn aren't alone in misdiagnosing the source of debt as something they contend governments can just run up, as opposed to the debt as something that extraordinarily exacting markets facilitate.

As is the case with Riedl, Rampell, MacGuineas, Galston, and seemingly every other budget expert, Mitchell and Rahn are deficit hawks. And they're convinced the deficits signal doom. Consider Mitchell's own book from 2024 that he coauthored with Main Street Economics blogger Les Rubin: it's titled *The Greatest Ponzi Scheme on Earth: How the U.S. Can Avoid Economic Collapse*. They're all predicting an Armageddon that is of course belied by the debt itself, and expectations of future debt enabled by—yes—soaring revenues that the various hawks claim against all historical evidence and market logic is the answer to the alleged debt problem.

Which brings us back to the supply-siders. They don't worry about the debt as much, but in response to the CBO report, Stephen Moore told the *Washington Post* that "I think this is a very dangerous situation for our country, and I'm not even a debt-phobiac. I've done this for 40 years. That [CBO report] was the first one that really scared my pants off. There's no bending the curve down at all. It just keeps going up and up."

It's kind of an odd comment from Moore, a genuinely kind and energetic happy warrior who believes deeply in market signals. For Moore to say that debt projections scare his pants off is for him to say he's worried the markets are wrong about all debt. But at this point, that's not the point.

The real problem with Moore's analysis of the CBO report was what followed. Moore's solution, like that of Mitchell, Rahn, Riedl, Rampell, MacGuineas, et al. was the same, but with the Laffer Curve thrown into the mix. "You've got to get growth up, because growth is what creates the revenues that you need to catch up with the spending."[4] No, once again. The revenues are what enable the spending, but also the borrowing that can only happen insofar as tax revenues are expected to continue to climb.

So, while it's hopefully apparent by now how hopeless the budget argument has become, and without regard to ideology, ideally this chapter has brought clarity to readers who might have felt this book is in some way a defense of government spending and government debt. Once again, not at all.

At the same time, this book *does* clamor for reason about the national debt. That it signals investor optimism about America's future is too obvious for words. See who can borrow and who can't.

Arguably the heavier lift will come from the effort within this book to convince readers that the debt doesn't result from too little tax revenue collection as the various ideologies claim, nor does it result from too much spending as others claim endlessly. The debt is a logical consequence of too much tax revenue now, and the expectation of quite a bit more tax revenue in the future.

Which hopefully starts putting to bed the absurd, Krugman-ite view of debt that says the more of it, the better for the economy. Per Rampell, Krugman's ideological ally, government borrowing means "reduced resources available for other, honest borrowers." The money that government taxes and borrows comes from somewhere, and that somewhere is you, me, and the man behind the tree. Government borrowing is an obvious sign of prosperity, but lays a wet blanket on much greater prosperity as precious resources are extracted by governments and handed out in politicized fashion. In other words, Rampell happened on the horrors of government spending and debt in her zeal to take down Donald Trump while naturally not realizing she did.

All of which takes us to where we will close this chapter out. In her aforementioned column about Trump's civil fraud case, in addition to her assertion that Trump's borrowing might have come at the expense of other worthy borrowers, Rampell suggested "that bank executives might have turned a blind eye to Trump's fraud." The line contradicts itself. If bankers "turned a blind eye to Trump's fraud" as Rampell indicates she believes, then why would she also believe Trump committed an act of fraud? What Rampell's very own reasoning implies is that banks and other financial institutions doing business with Trump knew well whom they were dealing with, thus rendering the notion that Trump secured funds through fraudulent valuations hard to countenance. Only for Rampell to want it both ways.

Having made her contradictory case that Trump defrauded lenders in the same sentence in which she contends its bankers "might have turned a blind eye," she wrote that "maybe bank *executives* [her emphasis] were willing to overlook Trump's fraud, perhaps to reel in their 'whale' and get a fat bonus." Okay, but by Rampell's very own editorializing, Trump wasn't a whale, and he wasn't a whale because he'd fraudulently inflated the value of assets he was trying to borrow against. Taking it further, how could loans at lower rates of interest to someone attempting to defraud them earn bank *"executives"* a fat bonus? Naturally Rampell's not answering. Which is the point, or should be.

Money is once again ruthless, loaned money in particular. It must be paid back. That it must be reveals the folly of all the worry about debt, all while ignoring the real problem of too much tax revenue. The latter is the real problem, albeit one that is never discussed.

CHAPTER FOUR

Government Debt Doesn't Cause "Inflation"

> *Money doesn't pay for anything, never has, never will. It is an economic axiom as old as the hills that goods and services can be paid for only with goods and services.*
> —Albert Jay Nock

Ross Perot could have been the world's richest man, or one of them. But wait, some will say, the late Perot *was* one of the world's richest men. True, his Electronic Data Systems (EDS) made the entrepreneur a multibillionaire. The only thing is that Perot could have had so much more. Tens of billions more.

What's unfortunate is that five words deprived him of World's Richest Man status. What are they? "My people don't drive Cadillacs."[1]

For background, in the late 1970s, investment banking great Ken Langone was in the process of raising money for what became The Home Depot. Founded by two recently fired retail executives named Bernie Marcus and Arthur Blank, along with Langone, The Home Depot aimed to revolutionize home improvement through the provision of the market goods necessary to do just that.

In a chapter about government debt not causing inflation, can it be assumed that while searching for start-up funds that Marcus, Blank, and Langone were pursuing debt financing for The Home Depot?

Hopefully you know the answer by now, but in a book that is once again repetitive by design, *clown question*.

As Marcus explained in a 1999 business memoir that he co-authored with Blank, *Built from Scratch*, "no one believed we could do it."[2] And when no one believes in your future, there's no debt to be run up in the present. If The Home Depot was to get any kind of financing, it would be equity finance.

The problem was that Perot wasn't happy that Marcus was driving a Cadillac. The high-end, full-sized automobile fit the big and broad Marcus, and his expectation was that the new company would take over the payments on the four-year-old car from his old employer, Handy Dan's. The problem was Perot. Though he had agreed to purchase a 70 percent equity stake in The Home Depot for $2 million, he made plain to Marcus as they ironed out the details of his equity purchase that "My people don't drive Cadillacs."

In response to Perot's adamancy, Marcus refused the $2 million that he and Blank desperately needed. His reasoning was that if Perot would allow something as inconsequential as a car to hang him up, what would he be like to deal with in the future when big decisions had to be made? And so, the indefatigable and ever-optimistic Langone was sent out in search of less-intrusive investors for a retail concept that "no one" believed would succeed in the first place.

So, while Marcus, Perot, and The Home Depot will merit even more discussion toward chapter's end, Marcus's search for cash was very telling. What it crucially clarifies is that no one buys or sells with money, nor does anyone lend or borrow "money." Marcus didn't need money; rather, he needed what money could be exchanged for. We buy and sell with production, much as we lend and borrow production, much as we exchange equity for production. Money is just the agreement about value among producers that makes it possible for them to get goods and services in return for their production.

It's part of making the essential point that even if there had never been government treasuries, mints, or central banks, money would be everywhere in the world where there's production. Production by its very name is *money* in the very real sense that we produce goods, services, and labor to get goods, services, and labor. Governments were never needed to create or "manage" the units of accounts that we call "money" simply because money in circulation is as natural a market phenomenon as the goods, services, and labor that money facilitates the exchange of. Repeat it over and over again: production *is money*.

This is what wealth manager extraordinaire David Bahnsen means from his discussion of money in his 2024 book, *Full-Time*. He writes that "before any of us can be a source of demand, we must first be a source of supply."[3] Exactly. We produce goods, services and labor in order to get roughly equal amounts of all three back, which means we produce for money, or in the words of Bahnsen, we produce for "units of account" that "represent wealth only to the extent that they can be exchanged for goods and services."[4] Governments can produce "money," people in the private sector can produce "money" too, but producers ultimately decide what money actually circulates based on whether the money is acceptable to other producers, and if it "can be exchanged for goods and services."

Money exchanges represent the movement of goods, services, and labor. Applied to Marcus, Blank and The Home Depot, the initial funds that would come to the start-up (Marcus and Blank had initially told Langone they would need $25 million to get started[5]) in return for substantial equity in the company would pay for real market goods like cars (including Marcus's Cadillac), salaries (albeit very low salaries) for the early executives, health insurance for those executives, land on which the initial Home Depot location would be built, inventory—hopefully readers are catching on here.

It's all a reminder of what's not discussed enough: governments have no credit nor can they give it out. Credit is a consequence of production, as in money and credit wouldn't exist without production. Credit and financing are what people create, not what governments decree through central banks and so-called "easy money." As the business stories in this book hopefully make plain, there's no such thing as "easy money." The latter is the stuff of economists and academics, and is unrelated to actual business realities.

Seriously, what Marcus and Blank would have given to have been able to borrow $2 million at low rates, or even the famously high interest rates of the late 1970s, in lieu of exchanging so much of the equity in their company for $2 million. But since access to real money that can be exchanged for actual goods, services, and labor is so costly, they pursued the only kind of finance that would touch them: equity finance.

Which is a useful jumping-off point for government debt and its alleged implications for inflation. Economists from left and right believe government spending powers inflation—which on its face is odd. Inflation is a shrinkage of the unit of account, as in the monetary unit like the dollar. Why—knowing what you, the reader, now know about how difficult money is to attain, and how demanding those with title to money can be—would government debt cause inflation? Put differently, why would investors buy government debt that pays out currency income streams that exchange for less and less? Why indeed, though we're getting ahead of ourselves.

For now, it will just be reiterated that government spending is a consequence of government's ability to tax or borrow against private-sector production. To associate government spending or government debt with inflation reads as a non sequitur, but for the purposes of showing why it's a non sequitur it's useful to accept what passes for accepted wisdom. At least for a little bit.

In a *Washington Post* opinion piece from 2021, left-leaning economist and Democratic Party eminence Lawrence Summers wrote that he feared an "overheated economy" if President Biden's $1.9 trillion virus spending plan was passed. Summers's view was that the trillions would "set off inflationary pressures" from all the new consumer spending brought on by the government largesse.[6] Interesting here is that former Republican Senator Phil Gramm, surely no ideological twin of the Democrat in Summers, asserted much the same, that inflation under President Biden was, among other things, "driven by excess demand."[7] Summers plainly believes government spending is an economic accelerant when in reality it's the exact opposite; that is, unless readers want to believe that the centrally planned allocation of precious resources in politicized fashion is better for the economy than market-driven allocations of resources. In the past Gramm would have nodded along to the previous statement, but for reasons that remain a mystery he began spouting the conventional left-wing view that government spending adds to demand; the latter an explicit rejection of Say's Law and supply-side economics. Strange times, or something like that. Gramm joining hands with Summers in asserting government spending fosters "excess demand."

Except for one problem. Government cannot increase demand. Only production can increase it. Per the Nock quote that begins this chapter, per Bahnsen, per your author, and per common sense, demand always and everywhere follows production, or supply. Were it something else, we'd all be equal. And we'd all be equal simply because as humans our demands are unlimited.

Despite that, we all have varying amounts of possessions, with the rich generally in possession of a great deal more than the poor are. The disparity doesn't spring from luck, or changing weather patterns; rather, it's a function of the rich, by virtue of being rich, having produced more such that they can demand or consume more. Crucially, what is a logical truth about who can consume the most is also an empirical truth: the top two-fifths of earners in the United States account for roughly 60 percent of the spending in the United States, while the bottom two-fifths account for roughly 20 percent.[8]

Some will naturally point out that there are rich people and/or rich offspring who produced nothing but who nonetheless can spend wildly. Well, yes. They inherited the productive fruits of others that enabled the demand. The main thing we need to be clear about is that government can't increase the capacity of people to consume or demand as much as it can redistribute wealth already produced. This hopefully clarifies what should be clear: government can in no way increase "demand" in the economy; rather, it can only shift the consumptive fruits of production to others. Only production can increase demand, and government produces nothing. That it produces nothing exposes the flaw in the reasoning of Summers on the left, and Gramm on the right.

Lastly, on the demand question, some will say that government spending or borrowing "mobilizes" otherwise dormant capital. Except that it does not. Repeat it yet again: *production is demand*. Short of them stuffing it into coffee cans, the wealth that the productive don't spend doesn't disappear; rather, it's shifted to others with near-term consumptive desires, including entrepreneurs and businesses in need of goods, services, and labor necessary to start a business or expand one. Thinking back to Bernie Marcus and his cofounders at The Home Depot, they were in desperate search for unspent wealth that could be exchanged for goods, services, and labor. As Marcus described their incredibly challenging pursuit of funds, The Home Depot needed money "the way somebody dying of stab wounds needs blood in his veins."[9] Which is a reminder that government spending doesn't mobilize precious resources as much as it politicizes the allocation of resources at the expense of individuals like Marcus who are trying to reinvent the future of commerce.

It's all a long way of hopefully searing in the minds of readers that governments decidedly *cannot* increase demand or "inflation" with their spending and borrowing, but they can most certainly sap production and progress. In short, Summers and Gramm got things backward.

Which leads to government debt itself. Can the latter cause inflation? Economist Richard Rahn was introduced in the previous chapter, and he believes it can. He wrote in a 2024 column for the *Washington Times* that "If the government issues so many bonds that people no longer believe the government will ever pay them back after inflation, they will either demand higher real rates of interest or stop buying bonds."[10] In a *Washington Times* column from 2022, Rahn wrote that "deficits" and "inflation" go hand in hand, and that a clear inflation fix would be to "Stop any new deficit spending."[11]

To be clear, Rahn is not alone in saying government borrowing instigates inflation. Hoover Institution economist and prominent conservative John Cochrane has written much the same, with great frequency, including in a 2023 book *The Fiscal Theory of the Price Level*. To Cochrane, borrowing begets inflation. Explaining what he and most economists deem inflation, he asked in a 2024 piece for the *Hoover Digest*: "Where did inflation come from? Our government borrowed about $5 trillion and wrote people checks."[12] In an August 2023 opinion piece for the *Wall Street Journal*, Cochrane confidently asserted that he could see even more inflation in the future if "Washington wants to borrow, say, $10 trillion for more bailouts, stimulus, transfers and perhaps a real war."[13]

So, with it established that economists tie inflation to government borrowing, we can then see the obvious problem with such a theory. The theory espoused by both Rahn and Cochrane says that buyers of government debt enable government debt, and do so knowing full well that they'll be fleeced by the very inflation that their lending allegedly enables. In thinking about what Rahn and Cochrane purport, ask yourself what a government bond is but a claim on future income streams paid out by governments.

Which is a short way of pointing out what Cochrane, Rahn, and countless other economists are implicitly asserting: markets are a tad dense, or realistically a lot dense. That the investors who buy debt from governments issuing it in large amounts do so knowing full well that inflation will eviscerate their returns. Not only does such a belief suggest impressive market stupidity, but it ignores what readers of this book have already seen: that the markets for money are ferociously exacting. Those perceived as unable to pay back what's borrowed don't get to borrow. See Uber, Nvidia, see the U.S. Treasury before it established an ability to raise revenue in taxes, see The Home Depot in this chapter.

Inflation is once again a shrinkage of the monetary unit whereby the latter exchanges for less and less. Knowing as readers do by now that no one buys, sells, lends, or borrows with "money," can it really be true that rising government debt would cause inflation? It's mostly a clown question unless markets aren't markets. Put another way, if there were a direct correlation between government borrowing and inflation, there would be very little government borrowing. This isn't to say that governments don't devalue their currencies as a way to shrink their debt (they sometimes do), but to do so is the stuff of self-flagellation. Those who don't pay back monies borrowed—and inflation is the act of not paying back monies borrowed—pay for it in the marketplace through much more difficult borrowing conditions.

As Niall Ferguson explained it in his 2001 book, *The Cash Nexus*, "a fall in the price of a government's bonds can be interpreted as a 'vote' by the market against its fiscal policy, or against any policy which the market sees as increasing the likelihood of default, inflation, or depreciation."[14] Ferguson put it so well, but readers would most likely agree that he was stating an obvious truth that can be found in countless examples in business, among individuals, and among governments. No one puts money to work with the intent of not getting it back plus returns commensurate with the risk taken, yet Cochrane, Rahn, et al. want us to believe governments have lenders who are uncaring about what they get back. Except that such a view doesn't stand up to economic reality. Goodness, if a relatively piddling $2 million could have gotten Perot 70 percent of what became The Home Depot, can readers seriously believe that there's billions and trillions out there in search of government debt that, because it is government debt, will decline in value? Sorry, but it's a total clown question.

To see why further, simply travel back to the previous chapter and compare the total debt of Haiti and Russia to that of the United States. There's quite simply no comparison, and the fact that there's no comparison can't be explained away in simplistic fashion of the kind that the futures of Russia and Haiti exceed that of the United States, or that Haiti and Russia's apparent fiscal parsimony imbues both with lower inflation as far as the eye can see. More realistically, and logically, the United States can run up debt in much greater amounts than any other country because investors see its future as brighter than the others, plus they trust that the odds of a major dollar devaluation are much less likely; as in countries seen as much less likely to inflate can borrow a great deal more than those prone to devaluation. Again, another statement of the obvious.

Better yet, the above assertion's truth can be found in the United States itself. When the 1980s dawned, total U.S. debt was roughly $900 billion, yet the yield on the 10-year U.S. Treasury note was over 11 percent.[15] Fast-forward to 2025, and with the U.S. Treasury $36 trillion in arrears, the yield on the 10-year is 4.33 percent. Translated, the cost of U.S. borrowing has substantially declined alongside even more substantial increases in U.S. debt. And it's not just the United States. Take the Dutch as another example.

Ferguson writes that "Dutch yields fell steadily from above 8 percent in the 1580s to 5 percent in the 1630s, 3 percent in the 1670s and just 2.5 percent by the 1740s." Yet this was at a time of rising debt for the Dutch, thus "confirming that there is no automatic correlation between the absolute size of the debt and the yield on the bonds that constitute it."[16] If anything, Ferguson understated his case. As opposed to there being "no automatic correlation" between higher debt levels and rising yields, the actual correlation logically runs in the exact opposite direction. Those seen as creditworthy can borrow in ever larger amounts at ever lower rates, while there, yet again, aren't rates of interest high enough to compensate investors for backing those known to default either explicitly through nonpayment of debt or "implicitly" through devaluation.

Access to the debt window is about reputation, as in the perception of one's ability to get back what was loaned, plus a rate of interest reflecting risk. Investors demand interest payments from Treasury that are a great deal lower than that demanded nearly forty-five years ago, and all readers would need to know this truth could be found in—yes—the surge in borrowing from the U.S. Treasury.

Importantly, this market truth runs wholly counter to what economists generally believe, that borrowing leads to inflation. Not only does such a view trample on common sense (that investors would pile into securities that they'll lose money on), but it's also rather predictably belied by market realities. Just as a rise in borrowing costs is, per Ferguson, a "vote" against that country's fiscal policies and/or its future, so is a fall in a government's borrowing costs a vote in favor of its future. Without defending government spending or borrowing for even a second, the surge in the U.S. national debt from $900 billion in 1980 to $36 trillion in 2025 is, contra Cochrane, MacGuineas, Galston, Mitchell, Rahn, Riedl, Rampell, Wilford, et al., a resoundingly positive comment from the marketplace about the United States' economic future, and one that signals a relative lack of inflation.

Some readers might respond to this that the United States is different, that per twentieth-century French finance minister Valéry Giscard d'Estaing, the dollar's global hegemony (as in usage around the world) confers on the United States an "exorbitant privilege" that enables rampant borrowing. It's a popular reply, but also *utter nonsense*. While the dollar most certainly has its demerits, most notably that it has floated without definition since President Nixon and his Treasury abolished its commodity definition in 1971, its global usage is a market-informed function of global trust about it as a measure or medium of exchange such that it, in the words of Bahnsen, can be "exchanged for goods and services." If the trust in the dollar didn't exist, then the greenback wouldn't circulate globally.

What's true for the United States is also true for Switzerland. The Swiss franc is one of the most circulated currencies in the world, and it is simply because the franc is one of the most trusted currencies in the world. *Quick: a buyer comes to you eager to buy your house, your car, or the shirt on your back. Will you take Swiss francs or Argentine pesos?* You know the answer. You take francs because francs buy in the markets what Argentine pesos rather frequently don't even buy in Argentina. In other words, a purchase of a house or apartment in Buenos Aires would be completed exponentially quicker with Swiss francs relative to Argentine pesos; and that assumes you could buy a house at all with pesos. Markets are wise, and that they're wise exposes the folly of "exorbitant privilege." The latter gets things backward. Trusted money is broadly circulated and an essential medium for issued debt, as opposed to debt being a function of some amorphous notion like "privilege." Privilege is a consequence of trust in the markets, not something decreed by powerful governments.

Furthermore, the phrase "exorbitant privilege" is belied by Treasury yields themselves. Think back to 1980. Back then Treasury paid 11 percent to borrow quite a bit less. In 2025, Treasury pays quite a bit less to borrow quite a bit more. "Exorbitant privilege" once again isn't just decreed, nor is it a function of the Fed monetizing Treasury debt or "money printing" as some believe; rather, exorbitant privilege is a function of investor trust in the U.S. Treasury's ability to tax abundant production now, but an even greater ability to tax it in the future. To be clear, the U.S. national debt isn't the fault of central bankers or exorbitant privilege, nor is it a function of too little tax revenue intake (the Left), too much government spending and not enough taxation (right- and left-wing scolds), or not enough revenue-maximizing tax cuts (supply-side happy talkers); rather, it's a function of too much tax revenue now and the expectation of exponentially more in the future.

Applying all of this to inflation—which is crucially a shrinkage of the unit of account—nothing about inflation or the expectation of inflation correlates with more government borrowing. This is true of the twentieth- and twenty-first-century United States, but also yields on government bonds of the European powers in the nineteenth century. Between 1843 and 1871, Ferguson writes that yields on British government bonds were lower (meaning it cost Great Britain less to borrow) than for the other "great powers" (think France, Russia, Austria), and that was a function of the British pound being tied to gold. Since the income streams of British debt were much more trusted, the cost of its borrowing was much lower. Again, basic, highly logical stuff, albeit stuff that runs counter to the conventional wisdom that says government borrowing leads to inflationary breakouts.

This isn't to say that heavily indebted governments haven't devalued before. They have and they will. Rahn cites the most famous devaluation of all in the column in which he oddly asserts that more government borrowing leads to higher rates of interest for the debt-hungry government. In the column, Rahn notes that in the 1920s, Germany devalued the mark to four billionth of the dollar, and in doing so, wiped out its debt. There's no doubting Rahn's history, but there's heavy doubt of Rahn's analysis of the history. Simply stated, if countries tended to do as Germany did, or even a limp imitation of what Germany did, there would be very little country debt. Furthermore, empirical realities reveal how backward the notion is that more government debt leads to higher borrowing rates for the borrower. See the United States once again, and see the Dutch example from this chapter. Countries known to pay back monies borrowed can borrow in greater and greater amounts at lower rates, while those known to stiff their creditors either can't borrow at all or can borrow in very small amounts, usually in another country's currency.

Which is what Rahn's ally in Cochrane eventually had to conclude. Though he published a book in 2023 about the "fiscal theory of the price level," and which promoted his thesis that government borrowing causes inflation, he ultimately had to admit (on the book's jacket, no less!) that "Inflation breaks out when people don't expect the government to fully repay its debts." Well, yes. Inflation is a shrinkage of the unit of account, a devaluation, it's the ripping off of creditors. Settled science. But if it were thought that country borrowers could and *would* do as Cochrane and Rahn theorize, there would once again be little to no government debt.

It's a long way of saying that the theories about the meaning of rising government debt are rather bogus. Markets are a look into the future, and debt a very exacting look into the future given how difficult it is for anyone—whether individual, business, or government—to borrow. Low interest rates on government debt, and Treasury debt in particular, are a loud rejection of the theory about government debt causing inflation, and they're a near total rejection of Cochrane's "fiscal theory."

All of which brings us back to Ross Perot and his deep-seated belief that Bernie Marcus shouldn't drive a Cadillac since Perot's people did not. As previously mentioned, this proved a dealbreaker for Marcus such that he refused $2 million in equity financing that he desperately needed. Perot's adamancy cost the Texas billionaire in a very big way. As of 1999, when Marcus and Blank's memoir was published, Perot's initial stake would have been worth *$58 billion*,[17] thus rendering Perot one of the top two or three richest men in the world. Though that's only part of the story.

Perot's stance on Cadillacs was indicative of parsimony on his part, which means he wouldn't have needed the $58 billion to fund a grander lifestyle of any kind. This is important simply because The Home Depot's market cap in 2025 is $350 billion which, if the Perots had held on to their shares (Ross Perot died in 2019), the family would be worth $230 billion today in Home Depot shares alone!

Which leads to one final question: does The Home Depot that couldn't borrow under any circumstances in the late 1970s have any debt today? Clown question! Of course it does. What's prosperous, what's expected to pay back monies borrowed with ease, is a magnet for the kind of financing that doesn't require any exchanges of equity. Yes, debt *is a consequence of prosperity*.

As this book is being written in 2025, The Home Depot once again has a market cap of $350 billion and debt of *$53 billion*. Well, of course. The debt discussion has always been backward, as has been the parallel notion that debt leads to maneuvers (like devaluation) which make it possible for the debt not to be repaid. How could such smart people believe what is so belied by reality?

CHAPTER FIVE

Ronald Reagan's Tax Cuts Did Cause the Deficits, but Not for the Reasons You've Been Told

> *You must never lend any money to anybody unless they don't need it.*
> —Ogden Nash

It was 2012, and the Ben Bernanke–led Federal Reserve was naively trying to "stimulate" the economy by making the cost of borrowing costless. Except that the Fed could do no such thing. The only way to shrink the cost of borrowing is for the borrower to reveal an ability to pay back monies borrowed. It's odd that something so basic requires saying, but its saying is required.

Notable about Bernanke's attempt to trample on ferociously exacting markets is that he earned himself some pushback from Dallas Federal Reserve Bank president Richard Fisher. In a meeting of top Fed officials, Fisher relayed to Bernanke an anecdote from Texas Instruments (TI), that the technology giant was borrowing in the .45–1.6 percent range, only to buy TI shares that paid a 2.5 percent dividend. Fisher's point was that TI wasn't expanding or creating any jobs due to the borrowing rates laughably said to be a consequence of quantitative easing (QE); rather, it was borrowing the money to purchase TI shares.[18] About the latter, there's nothing wrong with buying one's shares on its face, but it's useful as a reminder that the Bernanke Fed's attempts to make credit plentiful for those that needed it, or wanted it, did not work.

Leaving aside Fisher's implied point that credit placed in the right hands would "create jobs," the bigger point was and is that TI could borrow at low rates of interest with or without the Fed. This was true in 2010 when its market cap was north of $20 billion, and it's true in 2025 when it can claim a market cap of $135 billion. What possesses the means to pay monies borrowed back can borrow in ever greater amounts.

Just the same, that which hasn't demonstrated the means to pay back monies borrowed can't borrow at all. See the early years of Nvidia, Uber, Nike, Whole Foods, The Home Depot, and on and on.

Which brings us to Elon Musk. Right at the time that TI was borrowing rather cheaply, thus befitting its status as a long-standing technology blue chip, Musk was in sad shape as he desperately tried to keep Tesla, SpaceX, and various other seemingly "impossible" ventures afloat. In other words, borrowing wasn't an option. By the 2010s, Tesla had become "the most shorted stock in history,"[19] and before that so desperate was Musk for cash to keep Tesla in business that the parents of his second wife, Talulah Riley, quite literally offered to mortgage their house to get Musk a few hundred thousand dollars.[20] That's how frantic Musk was at a time when TI could borrow so cheaply. Low interest rates are a consequence of prosperity, of one's perceived ability to pay money back, not decreed by central banks. Just don't tell central bankers that. Please read on.

Responding to Fisher, Bernanke gifted the world with one of the all-time great replies unwittingly meant to reveal the boundlessly obtuse conceit of economists. He answered with "I do want to urge you to not overweight the macroeconomic opinions of private-sector people who are not trained in economics."[21] An instant classic! And a reminder that economists believe their theories and models and equations can overrun actual market realities. Except that they can't. Credit is produced in the private sector, and its cost is set in the private sector, as the ease of borrowing for TI in concert with Musk's extreme difficulties reveals in bright colors.

The above is a good jumping-off point for a discussion of one aspect of the economic portion of Ronald Reagan's presidency, and in particular the budget deficits that grew while he was in office. It would be difficult to find a past economic scenario that was, and still is, so misunderstood. And the misunderstanding extends across the spectrum of economic ideologies. Let's start with the left, and superrich investor Steven Rattner.

Rattner, a former *New York Times* reporter, maintains a *Times* column in his second life as a top capital allocator. In 2017 he published a column in which he criticized the tax cuts signed into law by Reagan, and that included a reduction in the top rate of taxation from 70 percent to 50 percent. Rattner wasn't a fan of the Reagan tax plan—not surprisingly, given the left's discomfort with tax reductions thought to benefit the rich in any way. Yes, it's odd considering the enormous wealth of Rattner, and so many centi-millionaires and billionaires comfortable paying higher rates of taxation, but that's not the point.

The point for the purposes of this chapter is Rattner's expressed view about the impact of the Reagan tax cuts on the national debt. In Rattner's estimation, "the Reagan tax cut increased the budget deficit, helping elevate interest rates over 20 percent."[22] Let's start with the interest rate assertion before getting to the deficits. The rate argument was total nonsense. Readers already know this from the previous chapter. Amid soaring U.S. budgets deficits since 1980 in concert with rising national debt, interest rates on the U.S. Treasury's borrowing have fallen. Plummeted, if we're being realistic. Which isn't, but should be, a statement of the obvious.

Debt is a consequence of the perceived ability of the borrower to pay it back, which supports yet again the logical contention that as deficits and debt go up, borrowing costs are in decline to reflect the rising expectation that the debt will be repaid. Reduced to the absurd, assuming the central governments in Haiti, Peru, and Benin are capable of borrowing, they would pay interest rates quite a bit more than the United States does in return for the privilege of borrowing quite a bit less. Basic economics, basic math, logic, you name it.

Back to Rattner's confident assertions about what followed the Reagan tax cuts, quite the opposite happened. Deficits and debt most certainly soared during Reagan's presidency, and rates of interest (in general, but also on government debt) logically fell as a reflection of that rising debt. And those rates have continued to decline in the decades since, as evidenced by a roughly 4.33 percent yield on the 10-year Treasury note with the national debt at $36 trillion, versus 11 percent when national debt was $900 billion.

Yet there's still the deficit question, or comment. Rattner says the Reagan tax cuts resulted in deficits because, in his estimation, those tax cuts reduced the tax-revenue intake for the U.S. Treasury.

Notable about Rattner's viewpoint is that it's not just limited to left-of-center Democrats who have a vested interest in discrediting the Reagan-ite view of the economy. Take Megan McArdle, a right-of-center columnist for the *Washington Post*, and someone who tends to caucus with the libertarian wing of the right. Writing for the *Post* in 2024, McArdle was as blunt about the budgetary impact of the Reagan tax cuts as Rattner was in 2017. In McArdle's words, "President Reagan cut taxes and deficits soared." While McArdle believes it's "a mistake" for critics of tax cuts like Rattner to "treat the Laffer Curve as an irreverent joke," she too rejects the oft-expressed supply-side theory about the Reagan eighties that "it was possible to cut taxes without cutting spending."[23] In other words, McArdle on the right believes as does Rattner on the left that a lack of tax revenues born of tax cuts brought on the "Reagan deficits" that this chapter and book claim are *Reagan deficits*.

Except that McArdle and Rattner are wrong about the Reagan deficits. How could they be when this chapter's title begins with "Ronald Reagan's Tax Cuts Did Cause the Deficits"? It's a perfectly reasonable question, and it's perhaps best answered by a supply-sider in top standing with supply-siders, Steve Moore.

Responding to the popular view on the left and right that the Reagan tax cuts caused budget deficits, Moore's answer has long been a variation on what follows: "the Laffer Curve worked: Lower tax rates did generate more tax revenues at the federal, state and local levels. Federal tax collections rose from $500 billion in 1980 to $1 trillion in 1990."[24] To some, Moore's statistical point about federal tax revenues doubling under Reagan would settle the point, that the Reagan tax cuts in statistical fact *did not* cause budget deficits. It's a reasonable point of view, certainly a traditional point of view among supply-siders, but it's plainly insufficient as a way of understanding what actually happened in the 1980s, along with what *keeps* happening.

Still, Moore's retort to the Rattners and McArdles, who to varying degrees reject the Laffer Curve, rates thought. Why are Rattner and McArdle right about the Reagan tax cuts causing deficits, but wrong about a Laffer Curve that indicates rising tax revenues in response to the Reagan tax cuts? Weren't both Reagan and the great Arthur Laffer right, and by extension Moore and other supply-siders? To get to an answer requires a discussion of supply-side economics and the Laffer Curve that has sadly come to define supply-side economics among its biggest critics.

Up front, supply-side economics is *reality*. Underlying this school of economic thought is a theme that's been regularly expressed in this book: demand is a function of supply. *Always*. Without production, there quite simply is no demand, or consumption. This is an important distinction since the vast majority of economists believe consumption is what powers economic growth. Economists reveal the shallow nature of their profession through their near-monolithic worship of consumption.

They ignore that consumption is a consequence of economic growth, of production. Worse, they ignore that consumption mirrors production, and in ignoring this, they promote utter falsehoods about government spending and wealth redistribution "putting money in people's pockets," thus increasing demand, and by extension, economic growth.

No, government spending and wealth redistribution in no way increases demand simply because production is the only way to increase demand. Which is a reminder that government spending and wealth redistribution don't increase demand as much as they shift consumptive power into other hands.

True "supply-siders" don't even think about consumption. They don't mainly because it yet again mirrors production. In which case, supply-siders focus all their policy energies on reducing barriers to production: think taxes, regulations, tariffs on foreign goods, and unstable money. While it's hopefully self-evident that all are substantial constraints on production, it's useful to briefly discuss all four.

Taxes on income, for instance, amount to a penalty placed on production. We work to *get*, meaning we work for money that is exchangeable for goods and services, only for governments to arrogate to themselves a share of the money we work for so that they can *get* and redistribute access to goods and services.

With taxes, it's worth adding that there are no entrepreneurs, there's no business expansion, and there are no jobs, without savings. Without *unspent wealth*. This is important, simply because true supply-siders recognize that the biggest source of savings for entrepreneurs in pursuit of an idea, and businesses intent on expansion, is the rich. Precisely because they're rich, they can't always spend it all. And what they don't spend flows to entrepreneurs and established businesses in the form of savings and investment. In other words, supply-side tax cuts aren't designed to encourage the consumption that so excites most economists, and that requires no encouragement as is, but instead are meant to encourage the savings and investment without which there's no economic progress.

Considering regulation, supply-siders recognize that market forces, including the excruciating challenges related to attaining capital (which have been discussed quite a lot in this book) are regulation par excellence. The best kind. Regulation from governments is anti-production, and logically restrains production as individuals who wouldn't rate jobs in technology, film, finance, medicine, energy, or name your sector are empowered to foist rules on those who do rate jobs in the aforementioned sectors.

Regarding tariffs, production once again is consumption. Which means tariffs are a tax on production. Much worse, precisely because tariffs are meant to tax the purchases of foreign goods, the tariff-levying country cruelly stunts the natural economic evolution of its country whereby production of goods and services is divided up among as many people and machines around the world as possible. The global division of labor that tariffs exist to suffocate slows the global cooperation that leads to abundance, much cheaper abundance for the productive to access. But most *cruelly* of all, it slows the migration of talented people to the kind of work that most elevates their unique skills and intelligence, thus limiting the productivity of humans. Yes, tariffs are anti-production simply because they limit our ability to divide up production among people. Economic growth is defined not by what we do, but what we no longer need to do. As work is divided, we're freed of much that we used to do in ways that logically boost our productivity.

Money is a natural market phenomenon, simply because money's sole purpose is to facilitate exchange among producers, but also as a way for producers to transfer their excess production (think loans or investments) to those who need it in return for access to greater fruits of production in the near, and sometimes distant (think inheritance) future.

Crucial about money is that when it's not trusted, we're not exchanging as much with others, which means we're not dividing up as much work with others. More troublingly, untrustworthy money (think inflation, as in a shrinkage of the money *measure*) causes those with title to it to invest (or consume) in hard assets (think housing, art, rare artifacts, gold) representing wealth that *already exists* as a way of protecting the wealth that, if left in money, would lose exchangeable value due to the shrinkage. The problem with the latter is that economic progress (think Uber, Nvidia, The Home Depot, Tesla, SpaceX) is born of investment in the equities meant to discover wealth *that doesn't yet exist*.

Exactly because money is so ruthless, as this book has made plain over and over again, untrustworthy money results in the latter migrating into hard assets representing existing wealth, and as protection of existing wealth from currency uncertainty. In which case, let's call inflation a tax on discovery of new wealth, and by extension a huge tax on production.

Supply-side economics is once again an economic school of thought that is relentlessly focused on reducing barriers to production, hence this digression. The latter as previously mentioned requires another one, specifically into the Laffer Curve, a distraction from the brilliant truth of supply-side economics. About the previous assertion Arthur Laffer, for whom the Curve is named, would likely agree. A focus on the Curve ignores the true meaning of supply-side economics, and realistically perverts it.

Still, the Laffer Curve must be discussed so that readers can understand why Rattner and McArdle are incorrect about the Reagan tax cuts causing the "Reagan deficits" despite those tax cuts clearly causing them, and why Moore is similarly incorrect about the Reagan tax cuts not causing the "Reagan deficits" despite those tax cuts resulting in a 100 percent increase in federal revenues during the 1980s.

The Laffer Curve makes an important case that at a zero percent tax rate, a government will collect no revenues, just as it wouldn't collect any tax revenue if the tax rate were 100 percent. Laffer's point in the 1970s when, though memories conflict about whether the conversation occurred, he drew the "Curve" for Dick Cheney (yes, that Dick Cheney) on a cocktail napkin, was (and is) that in between zero and 100 percent taxation there are high and low rates of taxation that will achieve the same tax collection result. Laffer's goal, a laudable one, was to convince legislators to lean toward the lower rate of taxation versus the higher one in pursuit of tax revenues. The goal of politicians, then and now, was to take in government revenue. Laffer's curve merely pointed out that if the penalty on work that is an income tax is reduced, the incentive to work, produce, and save will grow, thus resulting in a bigger economy and a bigger tax base for government to collect more revenue from.

While supply-siders still dispute whether tax cuts "pay for themselves," the debate is silly. Why should tax cuts "pay for themselves" in the first place? It would and will be better if government takes in less, not more revenue. As this book has repeated, government spending is a huge tax on progress as precious resources are allocated in politicized fashion, instead of being allocated in market-driven fashion to the Ubers, Nvidias, and Amazons of tomorrow. Still, and in defense of supply-siders, politicians don't like the idea of declining tax revenues, only for supply-siders to make a case that tax cuts would reduce the cost of work, thus creating the incentive for more work, production, and saving, followed by more tax revenue attained at lower, work-and-production enhancing rates.

To all this, Moore would and did point out how right the supply-siders were. Tax revenues yet again doubled in the 1980s. Okay, but what about the deficits?

Moore and countless other supply-siders have long made a case that the deficits in the Reagan eighties had little to do with his tax cuts, and they continue to make a case that since reduced levels of taxation change productive behavior for the better, that tax cuts are not the same as tax revenue reductions. Supply-siders point to the Laffer Curve to make their case that well-designed tax cuts don't shrink tax revenues; rather, they expand them as the incentive to produce grows; and amid growing productivity, the amount of income to tax once again grows.

About their arguments, there's no disagreement here. While it will be argued in future chapters that the level of government spending is of much greater consequence to growth than tax rates, there's no arguing with supply-siders that tax cuts don't result in commensurately reduced government revenues. Incentives matter, and reduced penalties on work and investment most certainly wouldn't shrink production, and would logically enhance it. Plus there's that tax revenue number that Moore noted.

Of course, it's with the number where there's disagreement with those on the supply side. And it has nothing to do with the number's veracity. It's easy to Google tax revenue collection for the federal government, which confirms Moore's numbers.

So what's the problem? The problem is that *incentives matter*. It's that simple. While supply-siders point to tax revenue increases in concert with rising deficits to make their cases that government spending is the cause of deficits, they are blithely ignoring their own mantra about how "incentives matter." Yes they do, and as we've seen in this book over and over again, a revealed ability to collect revenue increases the incentive for those with title to money to lend to the entity revealing a greater ability to take in revenue.

This is true for individuals, businesses, and governments too. Unquestionably it's most true for governments. Think about it. While the fortunes of individuals change all the time, and they certainly do for individual businesses, governments have a perpetual legal right to the earnings of their citizens. Applied to revenue-maximizing tax cuts, or tax increases for that matter, that which increases a government's demonstrated ability to take in more tax revenue logically increases its ability to borrow.

All of which speaks to the earlier assertion in this chapter that the Reagan tax cuts were powerfully misunderstood, and still are to this day. Deficit scolds from the left and right are convinced, against all reason, that deficits are a consequence of not enough tax collection, while supply-side happy talkers believe deficits result from too much government spending. In their analysis, left, right, and happy talker all imply that a problem born of allegedly insufficient tax revenue is the source of the debt. Which explains why all three miss the point, and reveal a fundamental misunderstanding of debt.

It doesn't result from a lack of revenue in the here and now, and certainly doesn't result from the perception of looming tax revenue shortfalls. In reality, and as this book continues to argue, debt emerges from the perception that revenue intake is impressive now, and will become even more impressive in the future. Again, what's true for individuals and businesses is also true for governments.

The Reagan tax cuts occurred in concert with soaring economic growth, and while economic theorists can and will debate about what aspect of the Reagan economic policy mix most drove the prosperity, it's undeniable that the Reagan policies resulted in a doubling of Treasury's tax intake to record levels throughout the 1980s. The Laffer Curve was and is real, and supply-siders wouldn't just need the 1980s to prove it's real. At the same time, it was the soaring government revenues that supply-siders projected that created enhanced incentives for those with title to money to lend it to the United States.

So yes, the Reagan tax cuts *did* cause budget deficits and soaring national debt, albeit not for the reasons promoted by Reagan critics and supporters alike. Incentives matter, but they also work both ways. There was quite simply no way that soaring government revenues weren't going to be met with much greater ease of borrowing for the U.S. Treasury, and subsequent borrowing. And we've seen just that ever since. As Treasury revenues have grown, so have deficits and the national debt.

The only thing that hasn't grown is the cost of borrowing. Naturally the latter declined, which was and is a statement of the obvious made evident by soaring national debt.

Bringing it back to Musk, as readers no doubt know, the fortunes of Tesla (among other Musk companies) changed. And for the better. While Musk reached the point where he was asking friends and family (though not his then-wife's family) to liquidate a lot or a little to keep Tesla afloat given how ruthlessly investors with actual title to money were treating him, he eventually righted the ship.

As Walter Isaacson tells it in his biography of Musk, Tesla board members decided he would be paid $100 billion only if Tesla achieved an "extraordinarily aggressive set of targets, including a leap in the production numbers, revenue, and stock price." Notable about the parameters foisted on Musk, "There was widespread skepticism that he could reach the targets."[25]

Put another way, Musk's success in transforming a near-bankrupt Tesla that at various times could attract neither equity nor debt finance into a company with over $9 billion worth of debt set Musk up for a huge payday. As this book is written, Tesla can lay claim to a market cap greater than $800 billion, after which there's billions worth of debt to show for it. Companies worth that much have revealed impressive means of paying borrowed monies back.

Without defending governments, taxation, or government spending, in the 1980s the United States similarly demonstrated a present and future ability to pay back monies borrowed on the basis of soaring tax revenues and the expectation of more. Yes, once again, the Reagan tax cuts did bring about deficits run up at ever lower rates of interest precisely because they were part of a policy mix that very much correlated with economic growth, and growth correlates with rising government revenue that is the catalyst for more debt.

CHAPTER SIX

*No, Central Banks Cannot and
Do Not Finance Governments*

One product is always ultimately bought with another.
—Jean-Baptiste Say

Some anecdotes explain so much that they require frequent mention. Which is why it's a surprise (to your author, at least) that it's taken all the way to the beginning of chapter 6 of *The Deficit Delusion* to discuss then–*Wall Street Journal* columnist David Asman's 1992 trip to the Soviet Union. Asman was there to observe relative freedom in action after the death of the communist regime.

In Asman's remembering, it was as though the weather knew what the people knew, that they were finally free. There was an indescribable beauty to St. Petersburg's newly unlocked streets, and there was palpable happiness. The people could finally live as they wished.

Of particular relevance to this chapter, Asman watched as buskers, musicians, and magicians showcased their skills for passersby "in the shadow of the Winter Palace." Some dropped ruble notes in the hats laid out by performers, while some occasionally left performers a *U.S. dollar.* Regarding the U.S. currency circulating in the country which had been U.S.'s foremost enemy in the second half of the twentieth century, Asman reported that a "dollar causes an immediate halt to the performance while the performers thank the donor."[1] Well, yes.

While the ruble was the Soviet Union's official currency, and while it remains Russia's official currency to this day, not all money is *money*. Money is a medium of exchange, its "sole use" as Adam Smith long ago wrote is to "circulate consumable goods." Money exchanges represent the exchange of actual goods, services, and labor. And when people and businesses bring goods, services, and labor to the market, they won't just accept any form of money. And they won't because they logically want to *get* equal goods, services, and labor in return for what they bring to market. Simple stuff. As the Say quote that opens this chapter puts it, "One product is always ultimately bought with another." Demand is production.

Which speaks to the problem with the ruble then, and even now. Its value wasn't trusted in the old Soviet Union. The country rendered destitute by central planning was awash in rubles that had little practical application in the Soviet Union simply because those with goods, services, and labor on offer weren't very likely to take rubles in exchange for what they brought to the black market. To do so was the same as getting ripped off, of getting much less in return for more. Sorry, but markets (whether free or "black") are very smart, and exacting.

On the other hand, a dollar pulled from one's pocket, even in the old Soviet Union (before and after the fall of communism), naturally summoned more and much better goods, services, and labor. Which shouldn't be a revelation so long as there's acceptance that markets work. People always and everywhere produce to *get*. They would gladly hand over goods and services for dollars simply because those dollars would exchange for goods and services that the ruble would not. And more of those goods and services. Naturally, St. Petersburg's street performers stopped to thank those who dropped dollars in their hats. A dollar represented real access to the scant market goods that circulated in the former Soviet Union.

So, what was the difference between the dollar and ruble? Did the former have some kind of magic chip within it? No. Not at all. Money on its own is worthless. It gains value from its perception in the marketplace as a medium of exchange. Money is an *agreement about value*, or it's not. With the ruble there was little agreement about its exchangeable value (Bitcoin proponents, are you listening?), and since there wasn't, it was too risky for producers to accept in exchange for actual production. What would the producer get back? And while the dollar isn't as stable as it was when it had a fixed definition as 1/35th of an ounce of gold, it's still seen as money par excellence globally. Producers agree sufficiently about the value of the greenback such that it ably fosters exchange around the world.

Ironically, or perhaps not so ironically, what was true about the dollar in the Soviet Union in 1992 remains true today. Particularly as fighting began between Russia and Ukraine in 2022, the dollar became king in Russia. As the *New York Times* reported in 2022, Russian citizens were "swapping intelligence on where they could still get dollars."[2] Call the dollar "paper gold" for those outside the United States given its global acceptance. Particularly as Russians (and Ukrainians) were set to exit both countries to avoid the fighting, dollars in their pocket would render their migration outside their home countries quite a bit easier. Markets once again work. And it wasn't just in Russia.

Consider North Korea. Though the won is its official currency, *Washington Post* correspondent Anna Fifield reported in her 2019 book (*The Great Successor*) about Kim Jong-un that "Despite all sanctions, the U.S. dollar is still the preferred currency for North Korean businessmen since it's easiest to convert and spend."[3]

Whether it's Venezuela with its bolívar,[4] Iran with its rial (over 3,500 devaluations since 1971[5]), or the franc in the Democratic Republic of the Congo, the dollar is the currency of choice for any substantive exchanges in all three. See the number of devaluations in Iran over the decades to understand why. The local currency almost certainly ensures either the buyer or seller will get ripped off with every transaction; hence, the dollar circulates as a way of facilitating exchange that would otherwise be reduced to barter. All of which explains why those much discussed (and laughed about) 50 billion Zimbabwe dollar notes can most often be found in frames in the developed parts of the world, not in Zimbabwe cash registers. No one would transact with what is so worthless.

What's been written so far should provide clarity as we pivot to Argentina and closer to the subject of this chapter. There's a popular view that governments are funded by the proverbial "printing press" as monetary authorities and/or central banks print the local currency to pay the bills. The absurdity of such a view has hopefully already been made apparent by the dollar's status as the currency of choice in so many countries not the United States. To then pretend, as various schools of economic thought do, that countries can and do print government funding most certainly vandalizes reason.

On the left, this belief that governments are only limited by "money creation" is called Modern Monetary Theory (MMT). MMT proponents believe governments that issue their own currencies need never worry about running out of money, or going into market to borrow money. Why worry or borrow when you can print? In theory, the idea behind MMT is for governments to find the program or programs that need funding, and create the money to fund them. Ridiculous? Well, of course. Money buys nothing, only production does. Only real production is exchangeable for money actually accepted by other producers. This truth is missed by the MMT crowd.

Okay, but before readers on the right settle into resting smug face about MMT, consider the belief of Austrian School eminence Guido Hülsmann, who writes that "fiat money allows the government to take out loans to an unlimited extent because fiat money by definition can be produced without limitation, without commercial limitation or technological limitation, and can be produced in whatever amount is desired."[6] Please tell me the difference between MMT fabulists on the left and those from the free-market Austrian School on the right. Tick tock, tick tock.... The reality is that both schools of thought thoroughly insult markets and the forces that guide them in their presumption that government and the spending governments desire is only limited by the speed of the printing press employed by the central bank, monetary authority, or both.

Back to reality, for every buyer there's a seller. And the seller is selling with a desire to buy in commensurate amounts, or store value (saving) in commensurate amounts. Which means the seller is not going to take just *any currency*, and for obvious reasons. The notion of "money printing" as the source of demand presumes ferociously dumb producers willing to take any kind of money for goods offered, yet as the dollar's global circulation renders rather plain, markets and the producers who populate them aren't stupid. Actually, they're quite *ruthless*. See the dollar's global use once again, and see how difficult it is to borrow currencies that actually exchange for real goods and services in the marketplace.

Despite this, the warring ideologies persist with their simplicity. Most puzzling is how often it's the free market–leaning thinkers who are most prone to repeat these simplistic arguments. Take a 2024 piece published at the Foundation for Economic Education (FEE) about falling inflation in Argentina. The South American country famously elected as president a fiery libertarian by the name of Javier Milei in late 2023. Since government spending is a tax on freedom and progress, Milei wisely promised and quickly acted on spending cuts once in office. "Inflation" as measured in Argentina subsequently fell only for FEE to start publishing pieces claiming a correlation between the two.

The op-eds asserted that "inflation" is an "increase in money and credit." Except that it's not. Credit is real resources (trucks, tractors, desks, chairs, buildings, computers, labor, etc.), meaning it's produced, and production presumes a commensurate increase in exchange media (money) to facilitate the movement of the production. That's, for instance, why there's so much money and credit in Palo Alto, California, but so little in Pueblo, Colorado. It's not magic or dumb luck that money is where production is, after all, money in circulation is a reflection of production. They go together.

That the scholars at FEE mangle money, credit, and inflation perhaps isn't surprising when it's remembered that most everyone does. They, as so many do, tie increases in money and credit to inflation despite the two once again mirroring one another, and despite the belief about what causes inflation presuming yet again imaginary, ferociously dumb markets whereby those desirous of resources would borrow in order to attain costly title to money that exchanges for nothing. It only gets worse.

The same opinion piece at FEE asserted that inflation is a "consequence of excessive money printing due to unbalanced budgets caused by extravagant government spending."[7] Except that the description of how "unbalanced budgets" reveal themselves has little to do with how budgets become unbalanced. If we ignore (only for now) what an irrelevancy a balanced budget is, we can't ignore a persistent truth found in this book's pages that "unbalanced budgets" are not a function of too much government spending as much as they spring from too much government revenue now, and the expectation of much more revenue in the future, thus the borrowing. While government borrowing once again does not increase prosperity, it surely signals market-perceived prosperity rooted in an ability to pay back monies borrowed.

The reality is that most businesses can't borrow money, and realistically most governments can't either. Borrowing is an effect of a growing belief in the marketplace that the borrower has the present and future means to pay the money back. Therefore, focusing on spending as the cause of the debt is to miss the point, and it's to turn a blind eye to the very real problem of spending. The problem with the spending is the *spending*, not the debt, which is merely a comment on the rising creditworthiness of the borrower.

As for this borrowing driving "inflation" born of "money printing," could the good, normally market-reverent people of FEE really believe markets to be this incredibly obtuse? If the question reads as flippant, then so be it. As this book has made plain, those with title to money are ruthless. Yet the free-market thinkers at FEE would have their readers believe that buyers of government debt do so without regard to their financial health or returns as they pile into government debt that, if the individuals at FEE are to be believed, will be eviscerated by inflation.

Some will respond that it is not investors buying government debt; rather, it's central banks and monetary authorities "printing money" to buy their government's debt. This odd presumption raises so many questions, including why governments form central banks if they exist mainly to prop up governments? Why not just buy printing presses? Of course, the questions reveal the impressive vapidity of the presumptions within the free-market camp. They really want us to believe that a creation of government can meaningfully fund government?

More important for the purposes of this chapter, hopefully readers can see by now from the Soviet, Russian, North Korean, Venezuelan, and Iranian examples just how empty the analysis is not just from the free-market right, but also from the pro-government spending left. The warring economic schools once again believe that the only limiting factor for governments is the speed of the printing presses operated by central banks, but as readers of this book surely know by now, the much bigger—and real—limitations on governments are market forces and the ferocious nature of money itself. And the very real need of producers to *get* in return for what they bring to the market.

Please contemplate these basic truths about buyers and sellers getting products and services in return for their own products and services somehow interacting with governments supposedly funding their "unbalanced budgets" via "excessive spending" allegedly financed through so-called "money printing." The very notion! It's no surprise that MMT types on the left would harbor such disdain for markets, but the members of the right? Implicit in their analysis is that printing presses enable government without limits, and of crucial importance, that producers of goods and services would blithely take money printed by governments in exchange for their production. Except that they wouldn't, haven't, nor do they.

No doubt some on the right eager to justify their long-standing embrace of mindless "money printing" theories will say that the producers take the printed money, only to then be left holding the inflation bag of worthless money. But to respond in this fashion is for the free-market leaning to dig themselves an even bigger hole filled with contradictions. That's the case simply because markets once again aren't stupid. Precisely because they're *markets*, the producers who represent a substantial portion of the marketplace sniff out bad money long before governments do. That they do is so obvious it almost doesn't bear mentioning. And it can be found in the axiom that producers produce in order to *get*, and don't take kindly to getting ripped off. Yet the free-market right wants us to believe the actual marketplace is filled with fools who are routinely being duped by governments with freshly printed money in hand. It's impossible to write this without laughing.

After which, further evidence revealing the impressive absurdity of the view that budget deficits are inflationary (see Cochrane, Rahn, Summers, and Gramm from chapter 4), and frequently inflationary because they're funded via "money printing," can be found in the natural reaction not just of St. Petersburg's street performers to dollars vs. rubles, but also to the global truth that the U.S. dollar liquefies exchange in so many foreign countries, including Russia, Iran, Venezuela, the Democratic Republic of the Congo, Argentina, and many, many more.

The obvious problem is that the aforementioned FEE piece—which represents so much economic thought coming from the right today about central banks financing big government—literally expects readers to believe that while no Argentinean would take Argentine pesos for his or her car or house, that before Milei government grew and grew and grew based on the printing of an exchange medium that not even a sentient *Argentinean* would accept for anything of substantial value. No!

Precisely because markets are *markets*, the printing press as a way to fund government growth as far as the eye can see is a nonstarter. This truth is demonstrated by the fact that the dollar circulates the world as medium of exchange. That it does is a loud, flashing market signal that "money printing" as a form of a finance is a big lie. If it weren't a lie, then it's easy to contend that Asman wouldn't have witnessed freedom when he walked the streets and squares of St. Petersburg in 1992, and he wouldn't have simply because Gosbank (the old Soviet central bank) would have printed rubles sufficient to keep the Soviet Union afloat.

Free-market types routinely disdain the "fatal conceit" of central planners, and do so with good reason. At the same time, they're blind to their own conceits, including their belief that governments and central banks can "print money," and subsequently grow government as though market actors don't ruthlessly demand trusted money in return for their production, and as though those same market actors don't ruthlessly push out of circulation the very exchange media that, if used, would rip them off. No. The flow of money, yet again, signals the exchange of goods, services, and labor, which means that devalued, or heavily printed money tends to disappear from commerce and cash registers precisely due to its debased status.

Stated simply, since only products buy other products, only trusted, stable money will do when it comes to exchange. Thinking about this through the prism of the most famous devaluation ever, Germany's in the 1920s, the myth persists to this day that German marks devalued to less than a four-billionth of a dollar were "everywhere." No, not true. And for obvious reasons. While the imagery of a wheelbarrow full of marks persists to this day, one senses the marks weren't being brought to market; rather, they were on their way to a trash can as *litter*. The reality is that the mark had ceased to function as money simply because money always, always, always enables exchange of products for products. What's collapsing in value, or soaring can't serve in a monetary capacity.

Pivoting back to Argentina, as this is book is being written President Milei is as mentioned rightly being cheered for shrinking government spending, while puzzlingly being lionized for the spending reductions reducing inflation. Goodness, if anything government spending (and borrowing—see chapters 4 and 5) increases would most associate with a *lack of inflation* owing to the simple truth that trusted money is accepted by sellers (governments are buying goods, services and labor, no?), while devalued money isn't nearly as much.

As for Argentina's monetary officials "printing" the money to fund government consumption along with deficits meant to enable even more consumption, such a view yet again presumes impossibly dense markets full of sellers willing to take what's rapidly shrinking in value in exchange for real goods and services. The free-market crowd doesn't exactly cover itself in glory when it confidently asserts that "money printing" finances governments and their debts. Things only get more foolish from there.

Eager to restrain government growth in Argentina said to be a function of "money printing" central banks, market-leaning members of the right are calling for Argentina to "dollarize" whereby the U.S. dollar would become the official currency. At first glance, this move makes sense. The Argentine peso is not even trusted in Argentina, so why not adopt what is truly the world's currency?

The why not dollarize question will be answered soon, but first it should be said that such a move would in no way restrain the growth of Argentina's government. Think about it. If the dollar were the official currency of Argentina, it's only logical that government borrowing would be even easier as a reflection of global trust in dollars. Once again, and contra the consensus (think Rahn, Cochrane, et al.—chapter 4) that government borrowing encourages "inflation" through the impossibility of "excess demand," devaluation of the debt, or "money printing," the reality is that lenders want to be paid back. If anything, a dollarized Argentina would find it easier to borrow. Basic stuff. The consensus is backward.

Beyond that, policy experts hopeful that Argentina will jettison the serially devalued Argentine peso are continuously harassing Milei to "dollarize." Again, on its face, interesting. As this book has made plain, and this chapter in particular, the dollar is already the world's currency. Why not make official what is already the de facto currency?

The answer for why not can be found in what some readers are already understanding: while Milei can decree the dollar the official currency of Argentina, or perhaps pass a law, markets always have their say. In fact, Milei can decree the Thai baht the official currency of Argentina for all we care, but ultimately the markets will decide what politicians cannot. Which is a long way of saying that the only thing Milei can really do is get the government out of the way so that Argentineans are free to produce. That's it. After that, money in circulation will take care of itself, circulate freely as a reflection of production.

Despite what we've been told for decades by prominent economists from the monetarist, Austrian, Keynesian, and supply-side camps, governments, monetary authorities, and central banks (pick your poison) can't increase money in circulation, nor can they shrink it. Repeat the previous sentence over and over again.

With money that's actually used by producers, the simple, unspoken truth is that its circulation is *production determined*. Where there's production there's always "money" facilitating the movement of production as though placed there by an invisible hand. And where production is slight, there's very little money as a reflection of scant production.

Since we always and everywhere buy products, services, and labor with products, services, and labor, we know governmental attempts to meddle in the amount and cost of "money" are the definition of vain. Precisely because the producers without which there is no "money" want to attain equal products, services, and labor to that which they bring to market, governments don't need to spend even a second on so-called "money supply" and its cost any more than they need spend time planning the provision of goods, services, and labor. To repeat, where there are market goods, there's always money facilitating exchange of the production.

Yet as this is being written, policy experts are breathlessly telling Milei that he must "dollarize." Such a view is as foolhardy and pregnant with conceit as would be central planners telling Milei that he must plan what's produced in Argentina, and how much.

The Argentinean people are the market, and their desire to consume in return for their production will act as a natural regulator of the money that circulates there. If dollars are what the Argentine producers trust, then rest assured dollars will circulate in Argentina just as they do everywhere else in the world where there's production.

Crucial to the monetary state of affairs in Argentina, but also the United States, Canada, and the Democratic Republic of the Congo is that the money circulating isn't a policy choice as much as it's a *market condition*. There is production, hence there are frequently dollars.

All of which brings us to the close of this chapter. The presumption that central banks finance government and debt is a naive conceit that if governments just create paper, producers will eagerly line up to hand over real wealth for the paper. It cannot be stressed enough how foolhardy such a belief is.

Which is why the popular belief on the free-market right that the Federal Reserve is the principal financier of the U.S. Treasury is so disappointing. Can esteemed economists really believe what is so at odds with reason? Sadly, yes.

Take Veronique de Rugy, a card-carrying free-market, limited-government stalwart, but also unfortunately someone who has been scaremongering about deficits and the U.S. national debt for as long as she's been writing for the public. In a column published in *Reason* on July 4, 2024, de Rugy made what she would no doubt agree were her routine comments about the "crisis" awaiting us because of the rising debt, along with the unwillingness of the debt "doves" to engage in "substantive discussion and action." De Rugy added her oft-expressed belief that the "root causes of the debt crisis" are "a perfect storm of higher interest payments and the looming insolvency of Social Security and Medicare." The "root causes" will be addressed in coming chapters. For now, de Rugy's alarm is featured to provide readers with even more evidence of how one-note the deficit and debt crowd is, plus to address de Rugy's odd assertion that "The more the Treasury borrows from the Fed, the stronger the inflation pressures."[8]

Let's start with "inflation pressures." What could de Rugy mean? It's been said before, and it will be said again, that the nations most capable of borrowing naturally are the least likely to inflate. Basic economics. If they were thought to be prone to stiffing their creditors, they couldn't borrow.

Yet for the purposes of this chapter, de Rugy's assertion that Treasury borrows from the Fed to fund itself rates discussion. It's of a piece with the belief—against all reason—that governments borrow from creations of government to finance themselves. This has already been discussed in this chapter with Argentina. To believe it is an implied way for de Rugy to say that markets are consistently duped whereby governments could get their money from central banks, and that money printed aggressively would then find willing takers in the marketplace. No, such a view isn't serious.

More seriously, if the Fed were the U.S. Treasury's financier, then it certainly would be true that yields on U.S. Treasuries would be much higher to reflect the market's realization that the Treasury has been reduced to borrowing not in the marketplace, but from an alleged *other* in government. In other words, if the Fed were the Treasury's source of finance, this would reflect in crashing U.S. Treasury markets the world (it's the "world" because Treasuries are the most owned income streams in the world) over to reflect the fact that the world's biggest borrower is literally borrowing from itself not *because it can*, but because it has no lending options beyond the "printing press."

Except that contra de Rugy's odd suggestion that the Fed is literally acting as Treasury's lender of last resort, U.S. Treasury debt yields substantially lower than it did when the national debt was a fraction of what it is today. Which is the market's way of saying to de Rugy that unless she thinks markets as shockingly dense as her analysis implies, the U.S. debt situation is much better at $36 trillion owed than it was when Treasury merely owed $900 billion.

Does the Fed own Treasury debt? Well, of course it does. But it owns it and *can own it* in large amounts precisely because the whole world wants to own the dollar-denominated payments of the government representing the most prosperous country in the world. Federal Reserve ownership of Treasury debt is a certain *effect* of just how solvent Treasury is now, and is expected to be.

Which brings us to an Elon Musk anecdote with which we'll close this chapter. On December 13, 2021, *Time Magazine* named Musk "Person of the Year." Commenting on Twitter (it was Twitter then) about it, Sen. Elizabeth Warren quipped "Let's change the rigged tax code so the Person of the Year will actually pay taxes and stop freeloading off everyone else." In a response for the ages, Musk answered with "If you opened your eyes for 2 seconds, you would realize I will pay more taxes than any American in history this year. Don't spend it all at once . . . Oh wait you did already."[9]

While enjoying Musk's reply to Warren, it's useful to look at it for reasons beyond joy in Musk's undeniable wit. The $11 billion he handed over to the Treasury in record tax fashion loudly explains why Treasury can borrow so much now, and why it will continue to borrow so much. Central banks don't and logically can't finance governments and their borrowing, but governments with access to the wealth of the world's most productive people can borrow, and can do so with ease.

What's true for individuals and businesses is true for governments too. Unquestionably it's most true for governments. Think about it. While the fortunes of individuals change all the time, and they certainly do for businesses, governments have a perpetual legal right to the earnings of their most productive citizens. Applied to revenue-maximizing tax cuts, or tax increases for that matter, that which increases a government's demonstrated ability to take in more tax revenue logically increases its ability to borrow. Central banks don't finance governments, and the Fed most certainly doesn't finance the U.S. Treasury as de Rugy et al. so puzzlingly assert, but excessive taxation of the productive most certainly finances government to our everlasting detriment.

CHAPTER SEVEN

Government Spending Is the Biggest, Most Progress-Restraining Tax of Them All

> *Capitals are increased by parsimony, and diminished by prodigality and misconduct.*
> —Adam Smith, *The Wealth of Nations*, p. 367

When pop singer Michael Jackson died in 2009, he had debts totaling over $500 million. Yet as of 2024, Jackson's estate had eliminated all those debts. Surprised? You shouldn't be by now.

A brief discussion of Jackson's debt story begins this chapter as more evidence that debt, particularly debt in large amounts, is a consequence of prosperity. Since Jackson earned in enormous amounts, and was expected to earn a great deal more in the future, he could borrow a great deal. Much as governments can borrow in greater amounts as their tax-collecting prowess grows, so can individuals and businesses as their capacity to earn grows.

Thinking more about individuals: what is your credit card borrowing limit? Particularly if you're an older reader, it's no reach to say that what credit-card issuers allow you to borrow now is quite a bit more than it was when you were twenty-one. Which is hardly an insight. Younger borrowers have lower incomes, less income history, and almost certainly have less history when it comes to paying off debts. Markets adjust to these realities. Only among pundits and academics is money ever "easy." Away from academics and those who write like academics, access to money that actually commands goods, services, and labor springs from a demonstrated ability to produce desirable goods, services, and labor. Jackson personified the latter.

It's not just that he had some of the biggest-selling albums of all time on his résumé, Jackson was still a popular performer (when he died he was training for a 50-show "residency" in England), plus Jackson (among other assets) owned the majority of the Beatles' song catalog, which he purchased for $47.5 million in 1985.

About the Beatles' catalog, the *New York Times* reported in 2024 that Jackson had previously sold a half share of it to Sony/ATV Music, only for the Jackson estate to sell the other half to Sony/ATV in 2016 for $750 million.[1] As readers can see, Jackson's ability to pay back monies borrowed was rather apparent. Again, none of this is surprising. If money is ruthless—and it is—it's particularly ruthless when individuals, businesses, and governments are attempting to borrow in large amounts.

Through Jackson, readers can hopefully see that just as his half billion in debts was a certain function of the capability to pay his creditors back, so is Treasury's debt of $36 trillion. Precisely because it positively dwarfs what Jackson owed upon death, the size is indicative of how much the markets trust the Treasury's ability to rather easily pay its own debts: not only does the Treasury take in staggering amounts of money now, but the expectation for the future is that today's collections look small compared to what's ahead.

Yet there's more to the Jackson story. Consider why he had so much debt. The aforementioned *Times* report indicates the singer "was famous for his lavish lifestyle and spent money with abandon," which included "a penchant for expensive art, jewelry and private jets." Jackson wasn't thrifty.

That he wasn't doesn't dishonor him. It's about freedom, after all. Furthermore, his genius earned him the money. At the same time, it can be said that Jackson's spending at the expense of saving didn't increase the base of available capital. As has been discussed throughout this book, entrepreneurs and businesses can't invent an all-new future or enhance the creation of goods and services at lower costs without capital. While production is consumption, one of the great things about the rich is that precisely because they're rich, they not infrequently have enormous amounts of *unspent wealth* that can be directed to entrepreneurs and businesses in pursuit of innovations and greater productivity born of providing employees the resources necessary to powerfully increase production.

See the Adam Smith quote that begins this chapter for a pithy explanation of the basic economic truth being described here. Capitals are increased by parsimony or, some would say, by a desire among savers to expand their wealth through the exposure of it to the stock market, private equity, loans, venture capital, and myriad other ways of putting unspent wealth to work. Without unspent wealth, there quite simply is no progress simply because there's no *discovery*.

The great George Gilder describes the discovery process wonderfully in his 2023 book, *Life after Capitalism*. In the book, Gilder doesn't at all disdain capitalism; rather, he asks readers to think differently about what drives prosperity within a profit-motivated, capitalistic system. In particular, Gilder crucially describes wealth as *information*. As he notes early on, "The material basis of the silicon economy," meaning the economy so responsible for great economic leaps globally, is "opaque and transparent, silicon chips and silica fiber optic lines, is sand."[2] In other words, what constitutes so much of technological progress is on its own worthless. What makes it valuable is knowledge.

Gilder's broad and crucial point is that everything we have on earth today, from cars, to airplanes, to cancer cures, to *supercomputers* that sit in our pockets, is comprised of material inputs that have existed for as long as Earth has existed. The difference between now and 4.6 billion years ago is *knowledge*. Thanks to endless experimentation conducted over billions of years, the knowledge we possess has skyrocketed, and with it, our wealth.

To clarify this, consider what happens when you arrive at the gas station to fill up your car. Oil and its by-products are of the earth, meaning for an overwhelming portion of humankind's existence, oil sat largely unused. And people suffered as a consequence. It's not just that oil is an input to so many consumer goods, it's that it enables the mechanization of so much work from the past that has freed humankind to pursue much more specialized work of all kinds that creates even more knowledge. Life before oil was so brutally cruel thanks to a great deal less in the way of material comforts, but much more importantly, it was horridly cruel because the lack of automation severely limited our ability to pursue the kind of work that amplifies the unique genius that resides within us all. But that's a digression.

Gilder asks readers to think more deeply about what's taking place when they arrive at a gas station. As he puts it, "when you insert your credit card into the gas pump, what you're really buying is the knowledge that makes that transaction possible."[3] Gasoline that powers cars didn't just happen, nor did cars just happen. What happened was that unspent wealth was matched with innovators bent on discovering an all-new future.

What's important is that discovering the future is expensive, and it frequently results in failure along the way. Think back to venture capitalist Peter Thiel's assertion from *Zero to One* in this book's introductory chapter: "Most venture-backed companies don't IPO or get acquired; most fail, usually soon after they start."

Looking back further in time, consider the Wright brothers, Orville and Wilbur. It was their unspent wealth from the bike shop they operated in Dayton, Ohio that made their pursuit of flight possible, a pursuit that was widely ridiculed. If readers want to forget a *Washington Post* editorial from the early part of the twentieth century that confidently asserted "It is a fact that man can't fly,"[4] they'll perhaps remember just how much the Wright brothers were ridiculed in their Dostoevskian attempts to prove the impossible. As the late historian David McCullough described in his 2015 biography of the brothers, appropriately titled *The Wright Brothers*, the "would-be 'conquerors of the air' and their strange or childish flying machines" served "as a continuous source of popular comic relief" to the wise. For one to be a flying enthusiast back then was for that same person to be "mocked as a crank, a crackpot,"[5] and seemingly with good reason. *Of course man couldn't fly* . . .

Thank goodness for the opposite thinkers, or in the words of Dostoevsky, the "extraordinary" who are willing to flout accepted wisdom. The challenge, as always, is for the different to find capital to pursue what is rejected as absurd, and frequently impossible. Except that it's more than that.

It's not just the discovery of the future that requires capital, it's the mass production that democratizes access to former luxuries that similarly does. Which requires a pivot to Adam Smith yet again. As he writes in The Wealth of Nations, "It is by means of an additional capital only, that the undertaker of any work can either provide his workmen with better machinery, or make a more proper distribution of employment among them."[6] Nothing has changed in the centuries since Smith reported on men working together in the eighteenth century, productivity skyrockets as the creation of goods and services is spread across more and more hands and machines. The latter is the basis of soaring specialization, soaring pay born of the specialization, and soaring living standards as cooperation among humankind and machines pushes down the cost of everything.

Which brings us a little bit closer to a discussion of where progress hasn't yet taken us. If it's accepted as inviolable that entrepreneurs and businesses can't innovate and mass-produce without access to capital, and if it's similarly accepted as inviolable that entrepreneurs and businesses must access wealth the productive don't consume in order to pursue their vision, we can then see the challenge of government spending. Governments have no resources, at which point the funds governments access through taxation to pursue their missions comes at the expense of savings and investment. There's really no getting around this simple statement of the obvious.

Consumption is always and everywhere a consequence of production, yet governments don't produce anything. At the same time they consume a great deal. And "great deal" understates it by many, many miles. A simple Google search indicates that federal spending in 2025 will amount to roughly $7.3 trillion. Tragic!

Economists will respond that the spending is actually a good thing. It "stimulates" growth because consumption stimulates growth. No, production *is* consumption. In other words, even without government or even with a federal government operating at a fraction of the cost of ours in the United States, there would be no decline in consumption.

At the same time, there would be a lot more unspent wealth sitting in the hands of those who actually produced it. What's unspent merely shifts the ability to consume into the hands of others, including, crucially, entrepreneurs and businesses in need of capital. Stop and think of all the precious wealth that the federal government wouldn't consume if it lived within constitutional limits, and by extension, think of all the wealth that would occasionally find its way to the extraordinary, along with those intent on mass-producing the visions of the extraordinary.

In short, the "unseen" of government spending is sick-inducing. Government consumption saps consumption precisely because it's a brutal tax on production. Remember the earlier chapters from this book and how difficult it was for Uber, Nvidia, Nike, and others to access capital. How many brilliant ideas never found commercial traction either because they couldn't find capital sufficient to continue operating? On this topic, David Parker, a benefactor of liberty causes, has referred to government spending as the creator of a "Museum of the Unseen" that grows and grows by the day. Government consumes so much wealth annually, so what knowledge pursuits and advances aren't happening as a consequence? It's scary to contemplate.

Thinking about governments mindlessly consuming the precious fruits of progress, it's something Adam Smith understood well. He cheered parsimony because he knew progress and freedom would be greatly muted if all we did was consume, or if governments consumed our wealth for us. Repeat it over and over again: consumption is the easy part. To consume is why we produce. But when we delay some of our consumption through saving, we provide resources to those striving mightily to move commerce forward. It calls for a repeat of the crucial truth that government spending not only *does not* increase consumption, it logically decreases it over time, because it occurs at the expense of savings and investment. As Smith argued, "When we compare, therefore, the state of the nation at two different periods, and find, that the annual produce of its land and labour is evidently greater at the latter than the former, that its lands are better cultivated, its manufacturers more numerous and more flourishing, and its trade more extensive, we may be assured that its capital must have increased during the interval between those two periods, and that more must have been added to it by the good conduct of some, than had been taken from it either by the private misconduct of others, *or by the public extravagance of government.*"[7] (Emphasis: mine).

Keynesian economists (a near redundancy) believe to a man and woman that consumption instigates economic activity, and this putting of the cart before the horse by the profession leads its members to believe that what matters is the consumption, period. Just spend the money without regard to how it's spent or invested. Which means Americans, but also people around the world, suffer mightily due to economic theory that says a shrinkage of the size and scope of government would devastate country economies globally, and by extension the world economy. No, what a backward view.

As this book endlessly repeats by design, consumption is what happens after production. In other words, governments can only spend insofar as they have abundant, taxable access to private production. Similarly, they can't borrow without abundant access to private production. Which hopefully clarifies a basic truth: government spending in the United States in no way boosts economic growth simply because it's an effect of economic growth. To then suggest, as economists confidently do, that government spending powers growth is to engage in double-counting of the kind that would make the most crooked of accountants blush. As for the debt, it doesn't stimulate economic growth as the Paul Krugmans of the world believe, and as modern supply-siders very sadly believe (see Phil Gramm et al. in chapter 4); rather, it's a function of growth that is way overtaxed.

Explained rather simply, government is arrogating to itself the right to the fruits of production only to hand the consumptive results of that production to others. Of course, there's a crucial distinction between governments spending our productive fruits or giving our productive fruits to others to consume: the actions of our federal government here in the United States and others around the world encourages prodigality (no one spends the money of others as cautiously or wisely as they do their own) at the expense of the capital without which the future can't be created and luxuries can't be mass-produced into common goods.

That's the case because government can't be an investor. About the previous assertion, it's not an ideological one. How could it be? Remarkable innovators in the United States self-identify as both Democrat and Republican. Looking back to the introduction, entrepreneurialism is not a choice or a political orientation but a state of mind. Some people quite simply think differently, or passionately see a way to achieve the impossible, only to pursue their vision with boundless energy. It isn't due to ideology that the government can't invest in these people, but because it's constrained by the *known* while entrepreneurs in particular are trying to take us to the *unknown*.

More challenging for government, where entrepreneurs aim to take us doesn't work nine times out of ten. See Peter Thiel et al. again. Can readers imagine the controversy of government directing taxpayer dollars to "impossible" notions operated by the "borderline crazy" and that fail the vast majority of the time? And while Social Security and Medicare will on their own rate a chapter in this book, further evidence that government can't play investor is rooted in the primitive nature of both programs. To be clear, this too is not an ideological point. Goodness, both political parties have supported the ongoing existence of Social Security for decades, despite it bleeding trillions on retirement accounts that return little to nothing for those paying into Social Security, and that, oh by the way, present and future recipients *do not own*.[8]

Which brings us to the biggest challenge—and horror—of government "investment." Nothing fails. See Social Security and Medicare again, but really, that's shooting fish in a crowded barrel. Better to just consider (or look up if you're unfamiliar) past Silicon Valley creations like Webvan, theglobe.com, eToys.com, and countless other creations of intrepid investment. To say they didn't make it is to waste words, and it is because most start-ups fail. And in failing, their precious land, mechanical, and physical (human) assets are released to better stewards of wealth. Stated simply, and referencing Thiel (Sebastian Mallaby too) from the introductory chapter once again, start-ups fail very quickly, to the economy's betterment.

Contrast this with the government. What's funded by government rarely dies, and for obvious reasons: programs quickly develop constituencies, and the power of constituencies grows as the spending on the program (and those employed by it) grows. This is true no matter the president in power, or who has the power of the purse. As Peter Baker (*New York Times*) and Susan Glasser (*New Yorker*) noted in their book about James A. Baker, *The Man Who Ran Washington*, even Ronald Reagan found shrinking government (what he was elected to do) very challenging. As Reagan's chief of staff, Baker saw up close that "every program" Reagan and his compatriots "wanted to cut had a constituency, it seemed, often including Republicans."[9]

Which is again basic evidence that government grows at the expense of progress. What can't succeed in the private sector fails, while what doesn't succeed in government proceeds to grow and grow. Still confused? Imagine the economic outlook today if instead of being allowed to fail, Webvan, theglobe.com, and ePets.com had been propped up, along with Blockbuster Video and Circuit City.

Taking the above further about the ruthless, pro-growth nature of money, let's briefly consider Silicon Valley–based venture capitalist Sean Jacobsohn. Within his home office is what's called a "Failure Museum." In this Museum there are Bear Stearns mugs, various BlackBerry devices, a WeWork thermos, cans of New Coke, and yes, there's a yet-to-be-opened bottle of champagne that was purchased for Webvan's IPO.[10] Is there a similar museum for shuttered government programs?

Some might respond to this that, as evidenced by the Failure Museum's existence, foolish spending is not just a government tendency—which would be correct. Government has no monopoly on foolish allocations of capital, but there is a major difference. Mistaken allocations in the private sector are corrected quickly, and subsequently exist as crucial information for those seeking knowledge. Better yet, failure in the private sector is an essential driver of progress.

To understand this better, it's useful to pivot back to George Gilder and *Life after Capitalism*. In it, he cites a story by his friend and Caltech professor of physics and engineering, Carver Mead. Mead recalls that his research group would stage its own version of "confession" in which failed experiments would be shared with other people. In Mead's words, "If it's a thing that doesn't fit, that's information. If it does what you thought, you haven't learned anything."[11] With government, even its failures don't teach us much simply because the endless throwing of good money at bad warps any finding.

Which explains why this book will not shoot fish in an even more crowded barrel, and talk about instances of government waste to make a case against government spending. If we ignore that there are numerous information sources and organizations dedicated to exposing examples of egregious waste, the view here is that such a focus misses the point. The problem with government spending is *government spending*. It's wealth extracted from the private sector, only to be handed out in a fashion that either encourages consumption or that warps research by divorcing the latter from the crucial discipline of the marketplace.

So, instead of giving readers a truncated version of government waste's greatest hits, it's better just to focus on how the highly successful operate in the private sector. Think Elon Musk. Regarding Musk, just mentioning his name might elicit a few snickers from readers who consider him a government supplicant. Please read on. It will be addressed.

For now, readers may or may not know that with SpaceX, Musk's aim was to bring market forces and discipline to a sector that had been calcified (the last Moon landing was in 1972) by too much government. With SpaceX, its customer would at times be government (sending supplies into space), but the capital at risk was that of SpaceX's shareholders. And SpaceX would only be paid if its rockets worked. In the words of Musk biographer Walter Isaacson, "There was a lot of money to be made if it [SpaceX] built a cost-efficient rocket that succeeded, and a lot of money to be lost if it failed." As Musk himself explained it, the parameters SpaceX works under reward "results rather than waste."[12]

Consider the way in which SpaceX builds its rockets. Isaacson notes that the exceedingly cost-conscious Musk "did not try to eliminate all possible risks. That would make SpaceX rockets as costly and late as those built by the government's bloated cost-plus contractors. So he demanded a chart showing every component, the cost of its raw materials, the cost that SpaceX was paying suppliers for it, and the name of the engineer responsible for getting the cost down."[13] Musk's thinking with the charts was to give his engineers ownership of the costs associated with rockets in order to bring the costs down. As he explained it, "If we don't end up adding back some parts later, we haven't deleted enough."[14]

Notable about this maniacal focus on costs and results is that SpaceX succeeded. Based on manpower alone, Isaacson reported that Musk and SpaceX made history with "the first privately built rocket to launch from the ground and reach orbit," and that he did it with five hundred employees. Boeing's division tasked with doing the same things as SpaceX had 50,000 workers.[15]

Yet there remains the comment that SpaceX, like Tesla, has been the recipient of government contracts and/or legislation favorable to the two. True, but Musk didn't nor does he write the rules. Politicians exist to meddle, including handing out favors. In which case, readers who choose to disdain Musk for being the recipient of government contracts, loans, and tax policy are directing their arrows in the wrong direction. In other words, you don't dislike Elon Musk; rather, you dislike big government. Consider yourself joined in that disdain by your author.

At the same time, don't forget that Musk's business story is one of him routinely innovating, and in the process founding companies routinely at risk of bankruptcy. To read the various business histories on Musk is to read about Musk pulling off miracle after miracle to keep his business ideas afloat. And as for SpaceX, the reality is that governments (including ours in the United States) desire a muscular presence in space. This was true long before Musk, and supports the basic truth that he didn't write the rules. So, with this being true, it's notable that, per his first biographer Ashlee Vance, Musk's SpaceX "can undercut its U.S. competitors—Boeing, Lockheed Martin, Orbital Sciences—on price by a ridiculous margin."[16]

Which hopefully underscores the crucial truth about government spending versus private-sector spending. With the former, waste that's a function of a lack of market discipline is a given, while with the latter, the ever-present fear of running out of money forces relentless effort directed at new, more efficient ways of doing things along with the trial-and-error discovery of new ideas altogether.

Too much throat-clearing up to this point? Fair enough, but it's important as a way of not distracting readers with "bright, shiny" instances of waste in favor of the much bigger problem: the extraction of precious resources from a ruthless-with-money private sector in favor of government consumption and allocation of resources in a fashion that annually rewards programs and agencies regardless of their value. Again, the problem with government spending is government spending, and that too isn't ideological if it can be remembered that the spending footprint has grown under both parties since the founding of the United States. Well, of course it has. See all the tax revenue enabling bigger and bigger government, along with how soaring revenue (and the expectation of more) has enabled even bigger government through borrowing.

In thinking about all this, stop and contemplate yet again what advances aren't taking place, what amazing businesses aren't being funded, what businesses are dying due to a lack of capital, and what jobs are not being created so that politicians can dole out precious wealth in politicized fashion. What aren't we accomplishing as a consequence of government? One way to answer this question is to consider paralysis. As with cars, computers, and microwave ovens, everything necessary to create all three has always existed, but for knowledge.

Which tells us that the resources necessary to render paralysis a problem of the rearview already exists. What doesn't exist, however, is the knowledge necessary to harness preexisting resources and human capacity to restore the ability to walk in the paralyzed.

The good news is that with each passing day, more and more is being learned by scientists on the way to a solution. As the *Washington Post*'s Daniel Gilbert reported in 2023, neurosurgeons "have implanted electronic devices into the brain and spinal cord of a paralyzed man that communicate wirelessly, enhancing his ability to walk and enabling him to climb stairs."[17] Wow! What else is there to say but wow!? Even robots have long possessed the gait of, well, robots, simply because the movements of humans are so *human*, and born of the wildly complicated machine that is the human body. It rendered curing paralysis the stuff of human flight, something that couldn't nor can it be done. An impossibility.

Yet scientists are now implanting devices in immobile humans that give them movement. It's hopefully a powerfully positive signal of what's ahead. As knowledge grows, so will the ability for doctors and scientists to bring mobility back to those who've lost it. The path to turning paralysis into yesterday's problem will be paved with endless mistakes that compound knowledge, on the way to actual fixes. Pneumonia and tuberculosis were humankind's cruelest killers in the nineteenth century, yet they're largely afterthoughts in the developed world today. Knowledge slayed what used to end life so quickly, and it's not unrealistic to suggest that particularly in the age of AI, knowledge compounded will render paralysis yesterday's fear.

All of which hopefully further lends credence to the basic truth that government spending is anti-knowledge. So much precious wealth is wasted in nonmarket fashion. Worse, and with borrowing in mind, consider the tax treatment when savers buy municipal bonds, or U.S. Treasuries. The income on "munis" is exempt at the federal, city, and state levels, while Treasury income is exempt from all state and local taxes. Just the same, if you risk your savings on doctors trying to discover a fix for paralysis or pancreatic cancer, two advances that would very much enrich those who discovered it, along with the investors who provided the capital, you'll face a large capital gains tax on the federal level along with whatever the state you reside in chooses to charge.

Regarding this state of affairs, where's the outrage? Not only does our federal government arrogate to itself substantial portions of our income through taxation, it also gives tax preference to its debt; debt that is already gilt-edged precisely because it pays out the most trusted income streams in the world: those produced by the American people, the most productive people in the world. Yet if you invest your wealth in private-sector initiatives meant to discover a better future, you face taxes on income from those investments, capital gains, estate taxes if your investment proves particularly successful, and on and on. To say there's something wrong with this picture would be an understatement.

Worse yet, consider the focus of the pundit class. Amid excessive government arrogation of our wealth through taxation, excessive taxation that enables abundant borrowing precisely because it's excessive, the free-market crowd remarkably changes the subject to deficit and debts. Think of the Cato Institute's Romina Boccia, its director of budget and entitlement policy. In a 2023 piece, Boccia wrote that "What's missing from the" spending and debt discussion "is serious consideration of the potentially catastrophic longer-term scenario the United States could face if spending and debt continue growing unabated."[18] Traveling back to chapter 1, conservative Jessica Riedl of the Manhattan Institute contends that "The federal government is sitting on a ticking time bomb." Left-of-center *Washington Post* columnist Catherine Rampell contends that a "fiscal reckoning could now be approaching," and then independent-leaning budget expert Maya MacGuineas can't talk to a reporter without predicting a debt crisis in the future. Can't they see how unserious their analysis is? Along with all the other analyses that parrots theirs, inspires theirs, or both? If you're a deficit "hawk" you, as a rule, think the "crisis" is a future notion when investors cut off governments. Really? Why?

To address Boccia—but realistically all the debt and deficit commentary featured in this book—what could she seriously mean by a "potentially catastrophic longer-term scenario the United States could face if spending and debt continue growing unabated"? Isn't Boccia missing something crucial? Aren't they all? Seriously, what isn't crisis-like about years, decades, and centuries of ever-growing government? Yet they're talking about the crisis of tomorrow? Sorry, that's backward. The crisis is long-standing simply because it began long ago with spending that grows and grows, and in doing so, saps the productivity of private initiative meant to fix all that's wrong, life-threatening, that isn't nearly advanced enough, and most important, what hasn't yet been thought of.

What's frustrating is that no doubt Boccia and others would acknowledge the problem of government spending, but even then they still miss the point. And they do because even those concerned about spending invariably pivot to the debt, "potentially catastrophic longer-term" scenarios, and then they laughably claim that all the spending is what causes the debt. It doesn't. What a nonsensical viewpoint, one that suggests *just anyone*,—any corporation or any government—can borrow. Sorry, but that's false and simplistic at the same time, while implying yet again ferocious stupidity on the part of markets. Debt is for the relatively few. Too much revenue now and in the future logically causes the debt, but the inevitable and routine pivot back to the debt means the self-proclaimed "responsible" in our midst are stepping on the real story, the unseen crisis of Americans (and the world) not progressing nearly as fast as they could precisely because government overtaxes us already, and the overtaxing enables ever more borrowing.

Despite too much tax revenue now and in the future looming large as the cause of so much debt, Boccia's colleague Ryan Bourne at the libertarian Cato Institute sees more revenue as the solution for the "debt problem." So does Riedl, so do left-of-center economic thinkers like William Galston and Catherine Rampell, and on and on. What an unfortunate distraction. Not only does the mere mention of "looming fiscal crisis" and "is there a way out the global debt crisis?" (Republican economists Dan Mitchell and Richard Rahn from chapter 3) presume enormous market stupidity, not only does it ignore a market verdict that says Treasury's debt position is worlds better at $36 trillion in debt versus $900 billion in 1980, it ignores the real problem of way too much tax revenue for government now, and quite a bit more in the future.

Again, the crisis is now. What copious amounts of life-enhancing and world-changing information do we not have as a consequence of government taking in way too much tax revenue? In short, the sin is not in how government gets our money (whether through taxes or borrowing); rather, the sin is in the extraction of wealth. The deficit hawks claim the crisis awaits, and it will involve debt, but the surest sign we don't have a debt crisis is the debt. Get it?

As for the "grandchildren" invariably cited by sanctimonious deficit hawks, the real burden for them is the size of government we're leaving behind for them, and the massive lack of progress that the latter vivifies. The debt? Yields on it continue to logically fall as a reflection of how certain investors are that Americans will produce the wealth to pay it back. The real crisis of too much revenue screams at us, but the alarmists of the various economic religions continue to drown out the screams with an odd focus on the *symptoms* of too much tax revenue collection, not the real tragedy of too much tax revenue collection.

CHAPTER EIGHT

If the Middle Classes Were Expected to Pay Back the Debt, There Would Be No Debt

We are blessed by the genius of the relatively few.
—Warren Brookes, *The Economy In Mind,* p. 77

In February 2024 the California Legislative Analyst's Office increased its deficit projections for the state to $73 billion. In response to the projection, an editorial in the right-leaning *Wall Street Journal* quipped that "Mr. Newsom has ambitions to reside in Washington, D.C., and based on his deficits it looks like he would fit right in."[1]

Asked about the budgetary shortfall by the *Washington Post*, Rob Stutzman, a California-based Republican strategist, noted that "It makes it hard to imagine why a California governor would be elected beyond California."[2] Writing a month later about a possible race to replace Joe Biden after Biden exited the 2024 election for president, George Will wrote in his own column for the *Post* that Newsom "should constantly murmur 'Thank God for Illinois,' the only state more disastrously misgoverned than his."[3]

About whether Newsom is a great, good, bad, or awful governor, this book won't comment. What's the point? Better to focus on the book's main subject, deficits and debt. California has a lot of both. Depending on where you look, total debt for the Golden State ranges from roughly $145 billion[4] to $1.6 trillion if you factor in unfunded liabilities, along with local government debt.[5]

By contrast, and the contrast is important for the purposes of this book, West Virginia runs annual budget deficits closer to $2 or $3 billion. Okay, what's the deal? Why are West Virginia's politicians so thrifty, and why are California's so spendthrift? Which is a question that if asked, would reveal in the questioner a substantial misunderstanding. Similarly, it would reveal misunderstanding if a Republican partisan were to note the difference between deficits and debt in the two states, only to conclude that Republicans (West Virginia now leans Republican) are thrifty with the money of their people.

More realistically, deficits and debt are a function of how many rich people cities, states, and countries are legally allowed to tax, along with how much wealth the rich have to tax. California has lots of rich people, and West Virginia doesn't. Without defending the spending or borrowing in either state at all, readers should know by now that the differences in total spending, deficits and debt between California and West Virginia can't be explained by ideology. And they can't be simply because politicians tax so that they can spend. No doubt politicians have different priorities, and surely different philosophies about government, but spending is what they do.

Think back to the previous chapter, and the discussion of Ronald Reagan. Reagan ran for president on a platform that including shrinking the size and scope of government, only for him to realize once in Washington that every program has a constituency, including Republican constituents. Just as individuals need no encouragement to consume, politicians need no encouragement to spend. That's why they're there. The arrival of money in the form of tax revenue is what instigates spending by politicians, and soaring tax revenue is what instigates investors eager for a safe, long-term income stream to direct even more money to politicians in the form of debt. The only limit to the spending of governments isn't central banks and their printing presses as the left-wing MMT and right-wing Austrian School crowds argue; rather, it is tax revenues, and what the markets expect in terms of future tax revenues given the impact the latter has on a government's ability to borrow.

California's "fiscal woes" will be returned to in a minute, and after a brief digression into taxes and who pays them. While there's the famous line about death and taxes as the only sure things, it should be said up front that when it comes to taxes, the *surer* thing is that the rich tend to foot the lion's share of the bill. And that's too bad.

As discussed in the previous chapter, the rich, by virtue of being rich, have the greatest capacity to save and invest. Capitals are increased by parsimony, or unspent wealth. It's because the rich generally can't consume all of their wealth that what they don't spend lifts us all. If you doubt this, consider that in the twentieth century the money behind venture capital and private equity investing largely came from families with names like Vanderbilt, Rockefeller, Whitney, Phipps, and Warburg.[6] As Rockefeller heir Laurance Rockefeller explained it in 1946, "What we want to do is the opposite of the old system of holding back capital until a field or an idea is proved completely safe, we are putting money into many underdeveloped areas."[7] In other words, those with immense, unspent wealth would fund the opposite of surething businesses; they are bent on trying things that most likely wouldn't work, but if they did ... Would these companies be funded with debt? Readers know. When the future is uncertain, and when future revenues are so uncertain as to be unexpected, equity finance invested by rich people with *money to lose* is the only way to go.

Not long after it opened its doors, fledgling sports network ESPN was near death, and likely would have died if investors for the Getty family hadn't discovered it and invested $10 million.[8] Precisely because the rich have money to lose, they quite uniquely drive progress born of investment in lots of interesting ideas that mostly fail (see Peter Thiel once again), but that occasionally lead to monumental discoveries.

Moreover, even the failures lead to crucial discoveries. As a consequence of becoming rich, the rich drive progress. And then once rich, their unspent wealth powers the crucial creation of even more of it. We overtax the rich to the detriment of our freedom and economic well-being, but also to the detriment of our health and technological advancement.

Back to who pays taxes, and its relevance to California's fiscal situation, it bears repeating that it's the rich. This is particularly true when the level of taxation is brought down. Looking back to 100 years ago, Presidents Harding and Coolidge worked with Congress to reduce rates of taxation four times, and in doing so brought the range of taxation from 4 to 73 percent down to 1.5 percent for the lowest earners and 25 percent for the highest earners. Subsequent to all this tax cutting, the percentage of total federal taxes paid by those earning above $100,000 rose from 28.8 percent in 1921 to 48.8 percent in 1925. Under this system of tax cutting the lowest earners saw their share of the federal tax burden decline 22.5 percent to 4.5 percent. As a *New York Times* editorial commented at the time, Treasury secretary Andrew Mellon "wants in reality to get more money out of [the rich] than they are now paying. But he proposes to do it by making their rate of taxation lower."[9]

The above statistics are being used in this chapter not to make a case for tax cuts as a way to raise more revenue, but actually to make a case that in reducing taxes on the rich, politicians are not reducing them *nearly enough*. That they're not is kind of a statement of the obvious. Politicians once again exist to spend, besides, imagine the "politics" of actually shrinking substantially what the rich hand over in taxes. Notwithstanding, it would be great politics in consideration of how much more capital would be put to work in market-driven fashion instead of by governments. One can dream.

Returning to who pays taxes yet again, it's worth pointing out that even Glenn Kessler, the *Washington Post*'s left-leaning "Fact Checker," acknowledges what's been said here about who pays the vast majority of taxes. Responding in January 2024 to then-President Biden's assertion that the average tax rate of U.S. billionaires was 8.5 percent, and that they weren't paying enough in taxes, Kessler noted that the top 1 percent of U.S. taxpayers account for more than 30 percent of all federal tax receipts. The *Wall Street Journal*'s editorial page cites an analysis from the Tax Foundation that says the top 1 percent of earners account for 25 percent of total U.S. earnings, "while paying 45.8% of total income taxes."[10] Back to Kessler, he reported that the "top 400 wealthiest taxpayers" paid an effective tax rate of 23.1 percent in 2014, and accounted on their own for 2 percent of total federal tax revenue collections. Regarding the previous number, Kessler pointed out that the "top 400 wealthiest taxpayers" paid more to the federal government "than the bottom 70 percent of taxpayers combined."[11]

Remember: we have deficits and debt because federal tax revenues are way too high now, and because they're expected to be much higher in the future. Looked at through the prism of who pays most taxes, we have deficits and debt because the rich are massively overtaxed now, and the ease of the Treasury borrowing now exists as a sign that the IRS will get even more out of them in the future. Forget about whether the effective tax rate is 8.5 percent, 10 percent, 20 percent, or even 50 percent, the simple truth is that even at 1 percent, the taxes taken from the rich and "top 400 wealthiest taxpayers" are going to dwarf those taken from middle and low earners, regardless of the rate charged them.

Which once again explains federal deficits and debt. Borrowing now is easy because the rich hand over so much in taxes now, and in the future they'll hand over exponentially more. As always, we can lament the progress lost because the rich are taxed so much, but also hopefully recognize that contra the warring economic religions, the sad, freedom- and economy-sapping fact that the rich pay too much in taxes now and will pay too much in taxes in the future explains the size of government now, the deficits now, the debt, and everything else. In other words, we don't have a problem of too little tax revenue (left and right, Rattner, Riedl, McArdle, Bourne, Boccia, Bandow, Galston, etc.), we don't face a dismal fiscal future (Mitchell, Rahn, etc.), nor is lowering the tax revenue through tax cuts (Steve Moore, most supply-siders) the answer to the size of government, deficits, and debt. All of it can be explained by wildly excessive taxation of the rich.

That California has a massive government, budget deficits, and debt is yet another statement of the obvious. Without defending or praising the governance of Gavin Newsom, to blame the deficit spending on him is a bit of a non sequitur. The main driver of the debt is that California is so full of talented people that it's a magnet for over 62 percent of total venture capital investment in the world,[12] those talented people backed with venture capital create some of the most valuable companies in the world (think Apple, Alphabet, Meta, Nvidia, Netflix, Broadcom, etc.), and the talented people backed by venture capital who create the world's most valuable companies are among the richest people in the world. Of course California has lots of debt.

Think back to chapter 5 on the Reagan tax cuts. Those reductions in the penalty placed on work most certainly did result in higher tax revenue collection for Treasury, the taxes were largely paid by the rich, but as has been shown throughout this book, rising earnings or tax collections attract investors who want to create income streams from those earnings and tax collections. Soaring tax revenue enabled much more borrowing. Incentives matter as the supply-siders tell us, and rising tax revenues create the incentive for savers to lend to the flush governmental entity.

What was and is true for the U.S. Treasury is true for California. As the aforementioned editorial in the *Wall Street Journal* (the one that made the quip about how Newsom would "fit right in" in Washington) reported, "the top 1 percent of California taxpayers pay about half of the state's income taxes."[13] Well, yes. There's your debt and deficit story.

Investors once again respond to incentives, and if you show them a state full of enterprising geniuses capable of creating enormous amounts of wealth, they're going to figure out a way to create low-risk income streams paid by those enterprising geniuses through their taxes.

Where it perhaps gets even more interesting, but surely not surprising to readers of this book, is that two years before the 2024 reports revealing a California budget deficit of $73 billion, the Golden State was taking in record tax revenue. No less than Governor Gavin Newsom said at the time that "No other state in American history has ever experienced a surplus as large as this."[14] Well, no. And no other state ever had such a budget "surplus" of that size simply because no other state has ever been populated with so many brilliant commercial minds.

What's truly awe-inspiring about what's taking place in California's economy is that its impact outside of California is so vast. Think about it. What is "technology" but advances that automate all manner of productive activity formerly handled by human beings? Which is why George Gilder confidently asserts that "Silicon technology is far and away the most important tool" of the $100 trillion global economy, "driving virtually all economic progress." Gilder believes rather persuasively that "Much of that the $100 trillion in GDP would disappear without it."[15]

Of course, wasteful government spending and debt in California is an obvious downside to the state's immense prosperity. Yet as with federal deficits and debt, the focus is on the symptoms (deficits and debt), rather than the real problem of too much tax revenue now, the expectation of exponentially more in the future, and then as this chapter hopefully makes plain, the unwillingness of politicians on the state and national level to do the one thing that would fix the government spending and borrowing problem: massively reduce taxation of the rich.

All of which brings us to the other broad theme of this chapter, that if the middle class were thought to be on the hook for all the federal debt, there would be no debt. Yet Manhattan Institute conservative Jessica Riedl believes otherwise. Think back to chapter 2. In it, Riedl is quoted defending a more muscular, better funded IRS. As she sees it, "we need this revenue," and that a failure to more aggressively fund the IRS "will ultimately drive up deficits and raise middle class taxes." Hmmm. That doesn't make sense. And the expectation here is that anyone who has read the book to this point knows why it's not true. But before explaining why what Riedl believes is not true, it's important to point out that she's not the only one who believes it. Dan Mitchell has said much the same, that "there are not enough rich people" to pay for all of the federal government's promises, and as such, anyone opposed to reforming spending "is unavoidably in favor of big tax increases on lower-income and middle-class Americans."[16]

Up front, the analysis of both Mitchell and Riedl presumes fully blind markets. To understand why, contemplate a classic line by nineteenth-century French political economist Frederic Bastiat, a thinker no doubt admired by both Mitchell and Riedl. Bastiat observed that "government is the great fiction, through which everybody endeavors to live at the expense of everybody else." No one reads the same book, but in this case your author understands Bastiat as saying government is *us*. We are its resources. Hence, it can be asked if middle earners, or in Mitchell's case, middle- and low-income earners, can borrow in size amounts of the trillions variety on their own? Hopefully the question answers itself.

The simple truth is that the borrowing capacity of the individuals who comprise lower and middle earners is limited precisely because they're low and middle earners. To then contend, as Mitchell and Riedl do, that government can borrow trillions based on its taxing power over lower and middle income earners insults reason.

Mitchell then adds that some of the debt can be paid for by "printing money," but that too suggests stupidity on the part of producers. As stated throughout this book, producers bring goods to market with an eye on attaining equal goods and services in return. They take "money" for what they bring to market to get what they desire. To then pretend they would be tricked by printed money that Mitchell himself claims doesn't trick him, is once again odd. It suggests producers work feverishly just to be ripped off. Not likely.

Furthermore, Mitchell's presumption about "money printing," like that of Veronique de Rugy in chapter 6 where she alleged that Treasury relies on the Fed for funds, ignores that if there were any truth to this, as in any truth that the printing press were Treasury's lender of last resort, it would be reflected in collapsing Treasury debt at all maturities to reflect Treasury's admission that it had run out of buyers of its debt. Much more important, Treasury markets would reflect the need to print *well ahead* of the printing presses being turned on. Markets anticipate. But that's a digression.

The more pertinent point is that middle- and lower-income earners do not face much higher taxes in the future to pay for all of Treasury debt. See Uber, Nvidia, The Home Depot, and Michael Jackson, along with the U.S. Treasury, California, and other high-debt locales. What enables debt is high individual earnings, corporate valuations, or governmental access to wealth produced by individuals and corporations. Without this demonstrated ability to produce lots of income or taxable wealth now and in the future, running up debt is a nonstarter.

See West Virginia's debt levels to better understand this truth, look up the wildly misguided 2021 Predatory Loan Prevention Act in Illinois to understand that low earners even struggle to get loans at rates as high as 36 percent, or just look to other countries like Russia and Haiti that are seen by investors as having less-than-prosperous futures. Low earners barely rate credit as individuals, which tells us they won't collectively enable major borrowing by their federal minders.

Money is ruthless. This can't be said often enough. Yet to read Mitchell and Riedl, and to believe them about where rates of taxation are heading, is to imagine that money is the opposite of ruthless and can be had easily. No, it can't. Put another way, if middle- and low-income earners were the future payers of Treasury debt thanks to looming tax increases, there quite simply wouldn't be much debt to pay off.

Chapter Nine

Low-Birthrate Hand-Wringing Reveals the Latent Keynes Within Economists

The only closed economy is the world economy.
—Robert Mundell

OpenAI CEO Sam Altman is part of an online "groupchat" that consists of business and technology luminaries. What most of us would give to be a part of these conversations!

What's most fascinating about these gatherings of remarkable minds concerns a bet they're in the middle of, and that will arguably be settled by the time you're reading this book. It involves "Unicorns" which, in Silicon Valley parlance, are companies that can claim $1 billion valuations.

The bet has to do with when the first one-man "Unicorn" will reveal itself. By one-man "Unicorn," Altman and friends are speculating how long it will take a business comprised of one person to achieve a valuation of $1 billion+.[1] Yes, you read that right. The very notion staggers the mind.

For so long, anything valued at $1 billion would have to be "big" simply because the value of a business is, per Peter Thiel, all the dollars it's expected to earn in its lifetime. So how could one person working alone create an operation capable of meeting the needs of so many people?

The answer to the question can be found in the expectations about AI, or artificial intelligence. Some refer to the latter as robots, or computers that will do and think for us. The preference here is to just refer to it as technology. That's what it is. As has already been discussed, technology is just an advance that automates away human effort, and increasingly human thought.

Which briefly brings us back to Vinod Khosla, the legendary venture capitalist who loves to back "impossible" ideas with investment. Let's call Khosla the Dostoevsky of his time given the Russian novelist's fascination with criminals" who go against the proverbial grain. At a 2023 conference put on by the *Wall Street Journal*, Khosla contended that within 10 years, AI will handle "80% of 80% of the jobs that exist today."[2] Here's your answer to the one-man "Unicorns" that are not too far off. Given the ability of machines to increasingly think and do for us, one man working alone will soon sufficiently possess the capabilities to meet and *lead* the needs of the marketplace in ways well beyond hundreds, thousands, and tens of thousands could in the past.

Just thinking about what's ahead, it's not unreasonable for readers to wish that they were just being born, or better yet, that their birth was years, decades, generations, or *centuries* away. And that's because present living standards in the developed world— now considered grand—are on the verge of being rendered remarkably primitive relative to what's ahead.

To see why, it's useful to think about the opening pages of *The Wealth of Nations*. Right away, Adam Smith opens up on a pin factory. (If you read my books and opinion pieces, chances are that you're more than familiar with this anecdote. Which is fine. It can't be written about enough.)

Smith observed that one man working alone in the factory could maybe, *maybe* produce one pin per day. But several men working together in concert with machines could produce *tens of thousands*.

It's a reminder that the only limit to the productivity of humans is related to their ability to divide up work with as many hands and machines as possible. The more we can divide up work in pursuit of increasingly narrow specialization that elevates our skills and intelligence in amazing ways, the more productive we can be as individuals.

These truths are plainly what Henry Ford deduced in the early part of the twentieth century. Eager to build cars for the "great multitude,"[3] Ford divided the work involved in their production across thousands of workers and machines. Assembly lines are a monument to individual specialization, and they become more sizable by the day.

Consider the recently discontinued Boeing 747. Those planes are a consequence of six million different parts manufactured around the world.[4] As always, the more we can work together, the farther out the production "frontier" is pushed. It's limitless, particularly in light of what Altman, Khosla, and others believe AI will do for us.

What your author would give to be able to present the bet of Altman and friends to Adam Smith. That is so simply because the work divided in a pin factory was early documentation of a story that grows in fabulousness by the day. While one man working alone could formerly not produce much at all, leaps in automation and mechanized thought have men working alone on the doorstep of creating billion-dollar companies.

The low-staffed but highly valued companies that will soon become commonplace are loud evidence that the productivity statistics produced by economists insult nonsense. The happy, incredibly bullish truth is that the babies being born today will quite literally be the productivity equivalent of hundreds of thousands of babies born in the not-too-distant past.

Yet despite this wonderfully bullish future, the pessimists are everywhere. They, if you can believe it, think the future is bleak because people are not having enough babies. In the 2017 words of then–*Wall*

Street Journal columnist Bret Stephens (now at the *New York Times*), "Lousy demographics means a lousy economy."[5] In 2015, Dan Mitchell wrote a blog post in which he told readers "I am scared." What scares him is that "Birthrates are falling" and the decline means "there won't be enough workers to finance the modern welfare state."[6]

Notable about all this pessimism and the present-tense nature of the description of it, is that it hasn't changed in the years since the referenced opinion pieces. In 2023, Mitchell continued to make his pessimistic case that there will be "very grim fiscal consequences" born of "Demographic Doom."[7] About Mitchell's relentless pessimism with regard to the ability of fewer babies to "finance the modern welfare state," it's no insight to point out that Mitchell doesn't believe people should reproduce just to pay for big government, and it's true that his solution is "entitlement reform," which will be discussed in the next chapter. But still . . .

The falling birthrates alarm is being rung from Republicans, supply-siders, and conservatives more broadly. It's not just Mitchell and Stephens. David Schweikert, a Republican congressman from Arizona, wrote in a 2024 opinion piece for *The Hill* that the United States' "declining fertility rate" signals "slower long-term economic growth and fewer options to finance mandatory spending programs financed by payroll taxes."[8]

Google most any right-leaning economist in particular, and you'll find commentary similar to that of Mitchell, Schweikert and Stephens. And it's not just the right-leaning. The falling birthrate "crisis" is like deficits and debt, something that has both sides fooled. Left-leaning Catherine Rampell, who can be found throughout this book, wrote in a 2024 opinion piece for the *Washington Post* that a "shrinking workforce can lead to stagnant or declining living standards, because workers power the economy." Rampell adds, à la Mitchell, that "a shrinking contingent of young people means fewer workers are available to care for the growing elderly population and pay for its retirement benefits."[9]

To be fair to Rampell too, this weird obsession with birthrates extends beyond debt and deficit hawks. Consider a revealing 2024 column by the great Monica Hesse at the *Washington Post*. Hesse compiled a truncated greatest hits of low-birthrate headlines including "America is uniquely ill-suited to handle a falling population" (*The Economist*), "The EU faces a major demographic decline" (*Euronews*), "Japan's Latest Plan To Reverse Declining Birthrate" (*Newsweek*), "South Korea's low birthrate budget needs an overhaul" (*Chosun Daily*), and then the *Wall Street Journal* ran an article with the headline "Suddenly There Aren't Enough Babies." Hesse's rather pertinent question is "why we should care about this population decline. Have studies shown that women and couples are happier if they have more children?"[10] But since this is an economics-focused book, Hesse's highly relevant question won't be asked.

Instead, it will simply be asked why we should care about this population decline? The question deserves airing because historians will quite simply marvel that something so obviously not a problem scared so many deep thinkers. While humans are most certainly capital in and of themselves, the automation of so much of what formerly required human effort means that the babies being born today will once again be the economic equivalent of hundreds of thousands of babies born in the past. As the predictions of Altman and friends make plain, the productivity of the near and distant future will render the present economically microscopic by comparison.

To this, some might reply that predictions don't always come true—which is true. But even now we're already witnessing the rise of billion-dollar businesses comprised of fewer and fewer employees. Think Kylie Jenner. At twenty-one she became the youngest self-made billionaire ever with her cosmetics company that consisted of seven full-time and five part-time employees.[11] While billion-dollar businesses of the past required major salesforces situated around the world, along with gargantuan marketing budgets necessary to help the salesforces reach potential customers, Jenner observed to *Forbes* that "I have such easy access to my fans and customers."[12] Something about hundreds of millions of followers on Instagram, Snapchat, and other social media shrinks the world and the cost of reaching the world in remarkable ways.

What's odd about this is that Mitchell in particular is a supply-sider. This bears mentioning because supply-siders routinely stress that human action isn't static, and specifically that tax cuts change the behavior of workers who are not static in their ability to produce. Well, yes, but what's true about humans vis-à-vis taxes is true about humans more broadly. We're not static creatures. Our capacity to produce continues to evolve. Just think of Jeff Bezos. He was born in 1964, but what if someone with his talents had been born in 1864? One guesses a smaller, much less connected world would have greatly limited his ability to create immense wealth. And then if Bezos were still to be born, in say 2064, imagine what someone of his genius could do then. Per supply-siders, we're not static creatures, but Mitchell and friends present gloomy outlooks about the future of the United States based on not enough babies.

In Mitchell's case, he doesn't just limit his pessimism to the United States Writing in 2024 during a teaching trip to China, Mitchell observed that "demographics" is "the biggest long-run challenge for Chinese policymakers." And why are falling birthrates a long-run challenge? It's the welfare-state thing again. Mitchell writes "that even a modest-sized welfare state is only feasible if there is a traditional population pyramid, featuring ever-larger cohorts of young workers to finance the benefits promised to older workers."[13] Yet again Mitchell obsesses about birthing to fund the welfare state, all the while writing as though human productivity is a static concept. Except that it's not, and we can see this clearly in China.

Consider Chinese billionaire Jack Ma and MYbank, a small business lender launched by Ma in 2015. MYbank has a 3-1-0 system that enables rapid-fire, collateral-free loans to businesses. By 3-1-0, MYbank tells its potential borrowers that they can complete a loan application online in three minutes, gain approval in one second, and crucially this process of attaining a business loan requires exactly *zero* human interaction.[14] Mitchell says China's economic future is bleak due to falling birthrates, but we can see with our own eyes that the Chinese presently living and who will eventually be living will see their productivity soar as machines increasingly think and do for them. In short, there's just no evidence supporting birthrate pessimism.

If China's not enough for readers, what about South Korea? The country's birthrate is among the lowest in the world,[15] and it's useful to add with sadness that South Korea can similarly claim the highest suicide rate in the industrialized world.[16] Yet despite these numbers, South Korea continues to prosper.

None of this is to say that rising fertility is a bad thing, but it is to say that falling birthrates logically correlate with rising prosperity. Well yes, of course. Birthrates were historically higher because in the nineteenth century a baby born even in the rich United States had as good a chance of dying as living[17], not to mention that in an agrarian age, lots of "hands" on the family farm was plainly the difference between eating and not eating. You can see this truth in India right now: in the agriculture-focused state of Bihar, India's poorest, the average woman will have three kids in her lifetime. Conversely in Tamil Nadu, a relatively well-to-do state populated with factories producing cars and iPhones, the average woman will have 1.8 kids.[18]

Contra Mitchell et al., a monstrous welfare state is most associated with falling birthrates simply because falling birthrates are most associated with the immense prosperity without which there aren't sufficient funds to finance a welfare state to begin with. In other words, Mitchell's argument that in the future, there won't be enough workers to "finance a modern welfare state" is as realistic as the one he makes about poor and middle earners paying off America's debts in the future.

Falling birthrates signal soaring taxable wealth now and in the future that will pay for abundant handouts while also easily paying off the debt so far accrued. As always, this argument is not meant to defend the welfare state (the view here is that it's more than unfortunate), but it is meant to correct the false notion promoted by economists, politicians, and pundits that falling production born of declining birthrates signals a bleak fiscal future for the United States that will be mopped up by poor and middle earners. No, not at all. Once again, if poor and middle earners were thought to be on the hook for government debt, there wouldn't be much debt or "dismal fiscal futures" for economists to scare their followers with.

The pessimism is wholly unwarranted and belied by market signals. If the Treasury faced a bleak future defined by an inability to stay current on debt of $36 trillion, then this would be reflected in the Treasury yields substantially higher than 11 percent, the amount the Treasury was charged to borrow back in 1980. Instead, the number is much, much lower to reflect market confidence that the most owned assets in the world (Treasuries) will make the owners of those assets largely whole.

Further considering the pessimism of so many Republican politicians, pundits, economists, and even supply-side types, what's odd is how very much the pessimism is rooted in Keynesian notions of how the world works. Consider how Rampell on the left and Mitchell on the right contend that the ability to finance the welfare state in the future is once again imperiled by a lack of babies. Implied in such a belief is that reduced procreation will reveal itself in reduced production (Mitchell) or consumption (Rampell) that will show up in slower economic growth, reduced tax revenue, and an impoverished welfare state.

The thinking informing such a view is totally bogus in and of itself. Many, if not most readers already know why it's bogus. But to refresh, consumption is always and everywhere preceded by production. No economic school can get around what is a very simple truth. And since production is what precedes consumption, we can say with confidence that fewer babies are poised to eventually produce on a level that will render present levels of production small by comparison. See Altman et al. yet again if you're confused. What they foresee solves the problems of reduced production suggested by Mitchell, along with reduced consumption suggested by Rampell.

Implied in both their arguments is that taxable consumption requires growing amounts of people, and that a declining number of people means less production, less consumption, and subsequently much less economic growth followed by reduced tax receipts. No, that's a Keynesian view of how economies grow. Production is production no matter the number of heads counted to achieve the production, it's set to skyrocket as fewer and fewer individuals are required to produce ever larger amounts of wealth, after which production itself is always, always, *always* mirrored by consumption of its fruits. Some of the consumption no doubt springs from savings and investment meant to happily multiply production's fruits, but it's still consumption directed at ever greater amounts of production. Tax revenues are an effect of economic growth, and soaring productivity signals soaring tax revenues collected from perhaps fewer individuals producing once again on a level of hundreds of thousands of individuals from the past.

Absent production, there's no way to consume unless those desirous of consuming have access to the fruits of production of others. If anyone doubts this simple truth, they need only refuse all work while refusing all aid from others. If they do, they'll quite simply lack the means to consume. Some may respond that humane Americans would never allow such a circumstance to last—to which the answer is, good. Yet even then, the aid provided would be a function of past production.

Applying this to Mitchell, his pessimism about the future financing of the welfare state puts the proverbial cart before the horse. Without once again defending the welfare state, its existence is a consequence of soaring wealth now that showers Congress with dollars, along with market expectations that wealth will reach exponentially greater heights in the future. Markets are wise. There's no chance the United States could continue to run up debts necessary to pay for a welfare state if the expectation were that the economy is set to shrink due to fewer workers in the decades ahead.

In short, this pessimism is rooted in a Keynesian view of the world that puts consumption at the top of the economic pyramid. No, consumption is a consequence of production and the size of U.S. Treasury debt today once again signals enormous market confidence that production in the future will dwarf that of the present. Welfare state funded. *Sadly.* The bitter fruits of way too much tax revenue now, and the expectation of much, much *more* tax revenue in the future.

Sam Altman and his "groupchat" friends would understand what's happening, as would Jack Ma in China. The babies being born today, tomorrow, and centuries from now will produce at levels many, many multiples greater than the present. Soaring U.S. deficits and debt are but a market signal confirming this.

Which is why contra Riedl, Wilford, MacGuineas, Rahn, Mitchell, Bandow, Schweikert, Rampell, and many others featured in this short book, we must not allow the political class to reform Social Security and Medicare. Yes, you read that right. No need to reread the sentence before the sentence before this one because it will be written again: we must *not* reform Social Security and Medicare. We must sit back and do nothing. To see why, please turn to this book's penultimate chapter.

CHAPTER TEN

Whatever You Do, Don't Let the Deficit "Hawks" Reform Social Security and Medicare!

> *Once something exists, it's rarely killed. Or even revisited. Killing things is often harder than creating them—that something has an owner and constituencies.*
> *—Jim VandeHei, Just the Good Stuff, p. 123*

In the spring of 1979, the great Manhattan Institute scholar John Tierney was covering "no nukes" protests for the now-defunct *Washington Star*. What struck Tierney was how many of the protesters had formerly been muscular players in the movement against the Vietnam War. Tierney wondered how it was that so many former anti-war protesters had so quickly become experts on the alleged horrors of nuclear power. Soon after, Tierney happened on the answer to the seeming riddle.

It seems this tendency among the passionate to jump from cause to cause actually has a name: the March of Dimes Syndrome. The March of Dimes was founded in the 1930s to fight polio, and it funded the vaccines necessary to help win the fight. Mission accomplished and organization shut down? Not so fast. After succeeding in the eradication of polio, March of Dimes morphed into an organization focused on preventing birth defects.

Tierney writes that nuclear accidents like Three Mile Island "offered new fund-raising opportunities and a new platform for veterans of the antiwar movement such as Jane Fonda and her husband Tom Hayden," who it turns out were in the crowd at the antinuclear rally that Tierney covered for the *Star* in 1979. Writing about the March of Dimes Syndrome for *City Journal* in 2024, Tierney observed that "For career activists, success is a threat. They can never declare mission accomplished."[1]

About what you've read so far, there's an obvious hole in the argument that Tierney would acknowledge. Precisely because March of Dimes succeeded in helping to eradicate polio, it's perhaps logical that it would pivot to other causes. The same could be said for Hayden, Fonda, et al., or for that matter the Manhattan Institute (MI), where Tierney hangs his hat. MI played a seminal role in bringing about saner governance in New York City after its struggles in the 1970s of the blackout and bankruptcy variety, so what a shame it would be if this Institute of powerful thought were to cease improving the terms of the policy debate.

At the same time, it's crucial to think about the meaning of March of Dimes Syndrome beyond the private sector. The good news about entities like MI, the antinuke movement, or any privately funded group is that since they're privately funded, the markets themselves will decide whether or not they've outlived their usefulness. With March of Dimes, it's apparent that its sources of support warranted more.

Which requires a turn to government. Government is ultimately filled with people who are self-interested just as those of us outside government are self-interested. At the same time, there's an important distinction: while private supporters of March of Dimes had the power to shut it down after the eradication of polio, government has *legal access* to the wealth produced in the private sector.

Since it does, it's much more difficult to sunset governmental initiatives. As taxpayers, we can't choose whether or not to pay our taxes, which means the size of the federal government grows in concert with the prosperity of the people whose wealth it has taxable access to. As this book has repeated with great frequency, the problem with the federal government in the United States in particular is that it enjoys way too much revenue now, and as demand for Treasury debt indicates, it will enjoy quite a bit more tax revenue in the future. The budget deficits and national debt are a symptom of the real problem that goes undiscussed within the various economic religions where the consensus thinking is that deficits and debt can only be fixed by a combination of tax increases and spending cuts. The thinking is backward, as readers should know by now.

Taking the difficulty of shuttering governmental initiatives further, it's also wildly challenging in light of what happens once government programs are seeded in Washington. To see why, think back yet again to chapter 7, and the passage from Peter Baker and Susan Glasser about what Ronald Reagan faced once in the White House: "every program" Reagan and his compatriots "wanted to cut had a constituency, it seemed, often including Republicans." If that's not enough, look back to the Jim VandeHei quote that begins this chapter.

VandeHei knows of what he speaks about how difficult it is to terminate government programs given his years as a White House reporter for *Roll Call*, the *Wall Street Journal*, and the *Washington Post*, but also from his deep understanding of Washington and its politics as cofounder of both *Politico* and *Axios*. "Killing things is often harder than creating them" due to the constituencies that develop around what's been created. The mission can never be accomplished, because accomplishment would perhaps signal that the bureaucracy has outlived its usefulness.

The obvious challenge is that bureaucracies, regardless of how effective they are, have employees who want job security. And in the case of Washington, they have politicians supporting them who similarly have a stake in their permanence. Big government amounts to a cushy retirement plan for politicians once they are out of office (and for family members while in office) as they get paid large sums to help move money and power in various directions. Worse, government once again is quite unlike private initiatives. With the latter, investors who fund them or donors who support them can always pull their support. And they do.

Consider Silicon Valley yet again and how quickly start-ups die. In contrast to the rapid bankruptcy of most technology start-ups, it cannot be stressed enough that no business or nonprofit ever runs out of money; rather, they run out of investor and/or donor support. If the business or mission is seen as worthy, the funding continues. If not, what no longer rates investment or funding goes away. That's not true with government, however, and readers hopefully know why it's not true.

Which brings us to this chapter's principal argument: whatever we do, let's not allow reform of Social Security and/or Medicare. Some will scoff at this notion for the reasons already expressed in this chapter: there's no killing or reforming what's already been created, and that's particularly true in government. Let's hope. Yes, you read that right, let's hope neither is reformed.

Of course, the obvious response to such a statement is surprise, or surely much worse. That is so because there's a consensus on the left and right that Social Security and Medicare must be reformed. As Ryan Bourne at the Cato Institute puts it, "almost all budget analysts" agree that a combination of more tax revenue and reform of the programs are necessary to fix a U.S. budgetary course that has us heading toward "crisis."[2] It's funny how market signals—including markets for U.S. Treasury debt—don't reflect the view of Bourne and "almost all budget analysts," but economists and budget experts tend to pay lip service to the genius of market signals only as long as those signals support their point of view.

Back to what "almost all budget analysts" agree about, it's not just market signals that contradict them. It's notable how little this consensus holds among those with power over the purse, along with Presidents who give the impression they have power over the purse. Congress has the spending power, but as evidenced by the growth of Social Security and Medicare over the decades, it at the very least loathes the politics of doing anything. Presidents generally don't want to touch it either. In his acceptance speech for the 2024 Republican presidential nomination Donald Trump attacked the Democrats for wanting to "destroy Social Security and Medicare."

In response to Trump's assertion, an editorial in the *Washington Post* observed that "In fact, neither party has shown much inclination to address the nation's looming debt crisis by adjusting entitlement programs in even modest ways."[3] The *Post* is right about both parties. As then-President Biden put it about proposed reforms, "if anyone tries to cut Social Security [or] Medicare, I'll stop them."[4] Leaving the views of Trump, Biden, Biden's replacement in Kamala Harris, and Department of Government Efficiency (DOGE) head Elon Musk ("the biggest Ponzi Scheme of all time," and "the big one to eliminate"),[5] the main point of the initial *Post* quote is to underscore the crucial point that the debt crisis narrative infects all the ideologies in a policy sense. It's accepted wisdom from all sides that a crisis awaits due to allegedly "unsustainable" entitlement programs.

By now readers are more than familiar with Manhattan Institute scholar Jessica Riedl and her pessimistic, we're a ticking time bomb, bleak view of what's ahead. Over and over again, in op-ed and article after op-ed and article, the conservative in Riedl calls for "ambitious reforms to Social Security, Medicare, and defense, as well as new taxes" to stop a "debt crisis" that she believes is coming "when the boomers retire."[6] Supply-sider Dan Mitchell writes of the need for entitlement reform as "The Unavoidable Choice: Entitlement Reform or Massive Middle-Class Tax Increases."[7] Back to Ryan Bourne at the libertarian Cato Institute, he essentially channels Riedl in his expressed belief that the way out of the alleged debt crisis is a binary of "raising tax revenues or cutting spending."[8] Bourne's Cato colleague Romina Boccia contends that "What's missing from the debate is serious consideration of the potentially catastrophic longer-term scenario the United States could face if spending and debt continue growing unabated,"[9] while longtime deficit hawk Maya MacGuineas asserts in pithy form that "the debt situation is unsustainable."[10]

What's important about the above quotes is that they're but a tiny sampling of a consensus that once again holds across ideologies: Social Security and Medicare account for a growing share of total federal spending, and as such, they're said by the allegedly warring ideologies to be the principal cause of all the deficits, debt, and a crisis that looms because of the debt. For a country that's said to be so polarized, there's little of that polarization found on the matter of the debt, and what to do about it. The conventional wisdom is that to avoid a "crisis," we must reform Social Security and Medicare.

Of course, the conventional wisdom is hopelessly wrong, which is no insight despite the sad fact that "almost all budget analysts" agree that the debt must be solved with more tax revenue and/or less spending. Those who agree with this widely held misapprehension should be pitied, for they know not what the problem is. Put another way, how can "almost all budget analysts" be right about what ails us if "almost all budget analysts" have mistaken symptoms (deficits and debt) for the real problem of way too much government revenue now, and exponentially more in the future? How indeed!

Alas, this book promised a different—and realistic—look at deficits and debt, so here you have it. What a shame it would be if those focused on the symptoms of too much tax revenue now and way too much tax revenue in the future were to succeed, against all odds, in achieving consensus in Congress for reforming the entitlement programs. If so, the last barriers to ever larger government would be irretrievably broken.

To see why, let's begin with a line from John F. Kennedy quoted by supply-sider Steve Moore. Moore regularly, and correctly, quotes

Kennedy as asserting in a speech made while president that "It is a paradoxical truth that tax rates are too high today and tax revenues are too low and the soundest way to raise the revenues in the long run is to cut the rates now."[11] What JFK observed, and what Moore so very much agrees with, is correct. Which is the problem.

As was pointed out in chapter 5, tax cuts for the rich are the best way to get more taxes paid from them. Tax cuts for the rich frequently lead to powerful economic growth (see the 1920s, 1960s, and 1980s), and more tax revenues. And to be clear, the tax cuts and economic growth merit loud cheering.

What doesn't merit loud cheering is that as evidenced by higher tax revenues born of the rich paying a lower tax rate on higher income and wealth is that government wins when the rich prosper. Put another way, truly brilliant tax cuts for the rich would be designed to ensure that they hand over much less as a way of ensuring that government doesn't win every time the enterprising prosper.

Bringing it back to the posthumous Kennedy tax cuts that followed the speech and line lionized by Moore, tax revenue and growth picked up in the aftermath of the tax cuts signed into law by Kennedy's successor in the White House, Lyndon Baines Johnson (LBJ). And from this unexpected revenue surge emerged Medicare.

About Medicare and the growth of government programs in the 1960s, it's essential to point out that this was the plan of the Democrats: cut taxes to grow the economy, and then use the extra revenues to fund more government. As top Kennedy adviser Walter Heller explained it, tax cuts generate "a better economic setting for financing a more generous program of federal expenditures."[12] Please stop and think about what Heller said, and what Kennedy said in concert with Heller, and what supply-siders have turned into their own argument: cut taxes to generate more growth and more government revenues that are a consequence of growth. Again, the freedom and growth part is great, but somehow supply-siders got duped into embracing an economic program explicitly meant to hand politicians the tax revenues (along with the ability to borrow against future revenues) necessary to grow the size and scope of government. In other words, supply-side gives with one hand in its present incarnation, but due to the movement's odd reverence for revenue-generating tax cuts, supply-side takes back with the other. Medicare instructs in this regard. Politicians respond to incentives like private-sector producers do, and revenue increases give them more money to spend alongside a greater ability to borrow. Tax cuts paradoxically lead to more debt, *not* due to falling revenues, but thanks to economic growth that results in more tax revenue along with a greater ability to borrow.

Medicare was signed into law by LBJ on July 30, 1965, as part of his "Great Society" program. LBJ spoke gleefully of the "seeds of compassion and duty which have today flowered into care for the sick." About LBJ's conceit, let the debate continue. What's less debatable is that Medicare was made possible by a surge of tax revenues that followed the Kennedy tax cuts.

Where it gets more interesting is that Medicare's budget in its first year was $3 billion. In 1967, the House Committee on Ways and Means rather optimistically forecast that Medicare would cost $12 billion by 1990. It seems those forecasts ignored what happens when services are offered by governments, and worse, what happens when the governments offering those services are annually showered with ever more tax revenue. As Pacific Research Institute president Sally Pipes reported in a July 30, 2015, opinion piece for the *Wall Street Journal*, Medicare costs had actually ballooned to $110 billion by 1990, $511 billion in 2014, after which Pipes projected $1 trillion by 2020.[13] Regarding the $1 trillion projection from Pipes, as of this writing we're not there yet, but we're close.

Like Medicare, Social Security similarly began small as a program to provide the elderly with sustenance, but also as a way to boost the economy by putting money in the pockets of people (elderly) prone to consume instead of save. In other words, economic theory was as bankrupt in 1935 (when the Social Security Act was passed) as it is now. Only production instigated by private savings and investment can boost the production known as economic growth, not the shifting of wealth from one set of hands to another.

Alas, this is not a book meant to dig into the details of Social Security, nor into the details of Medicare. Readers can guess your author's opinion of both based on what happens when governments centrally plan the provision of market goods, but a deeper discussion of this would detract from the purpose of this chapter.

What will be discussed, toward making a case against reform of either Social Security or Medicare, is that in 2024, and as is the case seemingly every year, it was announced in breathless fashion that Social Security would be "insolvent" by 2035. Which was and is an absurd projection. Such a projection firstly presumes that Americans have Social Security accounts with actual money in them somewhere in Washington. No, they don't. As 1960 Supreme Court case *Flemming v. Nestor* confirmed, Americans have no constitutional right to a Social Security account. In other words, we pay in and hope to be paid out a meager return.

So, without defending Social Security and its absurdly small payouts (in return for what we pay in) for even a second, the surest sign that the program is not remotely "insolvent" can paradoxically be found in the projections about its looming "insolvency" that annually excite the various deficit and budget "hawks" that you've read about in this book. Precisely because there's so little "money" in the mythical Social Security "trust fund," we all implicitly know that present and future payments will be made through general revenues to the U.S. Treasury. Yes, soaring tax revenues now and the expectation of much higher tax revenues in the future render Social Security payments as good as payments on Treasury debt which, as the low yields on that debt indicate, are seen by the marketplace as rather trustworthy. So again, without defending Social Security, it's easy to point out that its future isn't imperiled.

Despite this, and as the various quotes from this chapter reveal, a failure to reform these two entitlement programs has the "hawks" from the various economic religions up in arms. As ever, "crisis" to them isn't the extraction of so much in the way of precious resources by government now; rather, it's if and when the U.S. Treasury suddenly can't extract resources anymore. The "hawks" have been predicting this "tomorrow" for decades whereby Treasury can't borrow as easily as it can now (how this is a "crisis" has never been explained), with Treasury debt prices all the while mocking their alarmism. Yet they persist.

Where it gets comical is that in continuing to promote their alarmist narrative of "doom" in the future, proponents of reform unwittingly show us why their alarm is so misguided. Take Romina Boccia at the Cato Institute. She writes that "As entitlements consume a larger share of the budget, this exerts downward pressure on other budget priorities."[14] On the left, Catherine Rampell writes at the *Washington Post* that "Medicare and Social Security alone have already accounted for the majority of domestic spending growth in recent decades," and they'll "continue to crowd out future spending obligations in years ahead as the country ages and birthrates fall."[15]

To the parallel assertions of Boccia and Rampell, we should say "Hallelujah" while also asking them if they can promise us that their puzzling pessimism will reveal itself in government spending. Think about it. Government spending is misallocation of precious capital, it's waste, and to hear many on the right say it, it's all too frequently fraud. Most problematic of all, government spending amounts to the central planning of precious resources. If more and more of federal spending can be consumed by two programs, programs that are being worked around in the private sector as is, and as evidenced by the soaring wealth of elderly Americans, think of how many aspects of American life will not be touched by the enervating hand of government. Let the "crowding out" begin.

Boccia and Rampell opine as though government is capable of doing good things with wealth extracted from the private sector, but such a view presumes that the knowledge-pregnant private sector and life within it is improved by intervention from a knowledge-bereft government sector, and that Social Security and Medicare are restraining our government's ability to do more good things. Such a view isn't serious.

By extension, the view expressed by Boccia, Rampell, Riedl, Wilford, Mitchell, Rahn, MacGuineas, Galston, Bandow, and countless others, that we must reform Social Security and Medicare, presumes that if the two programs are shrunk, that the federal government will eagerly give the money back to the people. Which is *truly* unserious. Seriously, when in history has government in the United States or any country shrunk? Politicians exist to spend. That's why they're in Washington. They may have different priorities, but it ultimately comes back to what Ronald Reagan experienced when he was president: every program has constituents, and since they all do, politicians trade votes to make sure their "pets" are fed with copious funding. Which means reform followed by a return of the unspent funds is not happening.

Some will say that the money saved could pay off the debt, but this reveals yet again the confusion of the deficit "hawks" as is. Paying off the debt doesn't alter the cause of all the debt, which is too much tax revenue now and way too much in the future, which means paying off the debt is like paying off the credit card of a profligate borrower: it will just enable even more borrowing.

We can refute the notion that government would just give the money saved from reform back merely by observing the way government presently operates. This raises questions about the reasoning of Boccia in particular. She worries that Social Security and Medicare exert "downward pressure on other budget priorities," but that's once again a good thing. To see why, imagine what would happen after serious entitlement reform. Suddenly enormous amounts of tax revenue now and in the future are just waiting to be spent. To then presume that Congress wouldn't find new ways to spend those dollars brings new meaning to naivete.

Don't forget that Medicare started small, as did Social Security. The engine of growth for both was soaring federal revenues. So, while it's shooting fish in a barrel to say both entitlements were bad ideas, give them this: according to their fiercest critics they exert "downward pressure on other budget priorities" and new priorities altogether, thus restraining the rise of all new and wasteful programs that would only grow. Yes, keep Social Security and Medicare in place to suffocate the creation of their much worse, and eventually much more expensive replacements. *Do not* free up money for politicians.

Which brings us to the other major issue as this chapter comes to a close. Interest payments on the debt. Like the debt itself, this too excites the chorus of debt "hawks" who've made appearances throughout this book. On the subject of these interest payments, Catherine Rampell writes that "If interest costs rise and economic growth doesn't keep up, we'll have much less 'fiscal space' to commit to new programs."[16] From the right, Riedl similarly complained in October 2023 that interest payments "on the debt already doubled over the last two years, and are expected to double again over the next decade. Congress remains completely asleep at the wheel, and unwilling to make even minor gestures toward reining in the toxic combination of rising debt and higher interest rates."[17] At the *Wall Street Journal*'s editorial page, libertarian-leaning columnist Holman Jenkins writes with worry that "interest expense will soon outstrip $1.4 trillion in annual Social Security spending,"[18] and then at the Peter G. Peterson Foundation, CEO Michael Peterson told the *Washington Post* with evident worry in 2024 that "The harmful effects of higher interest rates fueling higher interest costs on a huge existing debt load are continuing, and leading to additional borrowing. It's the definition of unsustainable."[19]

The Peterson Foundation itself runs advertisements lamenting annual interest costs on the federal debt of $659 billion, which, per Holman Jenkins, are heading well above $1 trillion. These laments are indicative of how the various ideologies miss the point. They never talk about the fact that heavy interest payments—like enormous debt, deficits, and spending—are a symptom of way too much tax revenue now and the expectation of much, much more in the future. As always, there is ubiquitous focus and nail-biting about interest payments yet little-to-nothing about the massive extractions of private wealth from the economy in the present and future that make all the interest paid on the borrowing possible. To rephrase James Carville: "It's Too Much Revenue, Stupid!"

Furthermore, the hysteria about interest payments is, like the laments from Boccia and Rampell about entitlement spending exerting "downward pressure on other budget priorities," unwittingly an argument for maintenance of the status quo. If the rising cost of Social Security, Medicare, and interest on debt restrains government from expanding its footprint into other areas, isn't this a good thing? Paying interest on debt is just that (would it that most government spending globally was merely interest payments!), while not paying interest on debt due to reform once again arms politicians with fresh money that they would only be so happy to spend.

Going back to chapter 1, and Committee for a Responsible Federal Budget president Maya MacGuineas, she alleged that "The risks we run from this growing mountain of debt run the gamut from slower economic growth to lower incomes, an inability to respond to emergencies and a weaker role in the world." The expert gets it backward. Horrible as the spending and borrowing are, they're a signal of booming economic growth that the U.S. Treasury (and by extension, Congress) has too much control over, while the surest sign the debt isn't bringing on "lower incomes" is the debt itself. In other words, the debt is yet again a signal of how well-to-do Americans are. What would eventuate even higher incomes is less tax revenue finding its way to Washington and less borrowing, yet MacGuineas routinely argues for dialogue about "how to increase revenue." As for her lament about the debt leading to "an inability to respond to emergencies and a weaker role in the world," the view implies that the central planning of resource allocation that is a rather apt description of government spending is a positive during times of trouble. Sorry, but central planning, which never works in good times, hardly attains genius during the bad. Let's not encourage more of it.

Which explains yet again the title of this chapter, and the content within it. Government spending saps freedom and prosperity, period. Our federal government can spend massive amounts precisely because it collects way too much in taxes now and expects to take in much more in the future. Unfortunate as the latter is, it's at least mitigated by past errors of the Social Security and Medicare variety, two programs so expensive that they consume an ever-growing share of the budget along with interest payments meant to pay the debt run up to fund both. In this case, what's bad is good. Keep what the rational would rather not have (Social Security, Medicare, and enormous interest payments on debt) as barriers to Congress's ability to create programs that the rational would despise even more.

Conclusion

I only believe in my main ideal. It consists precisely in people being divided generally, according to the law of nature, into two categories: a lower or, so to speak, material category (the ordinary), serving solely for the reproduction of their own kind; and people proper—that is, those who have the gift or talent of speaking a new word in their environment.
—Fyodor Dostoevsky, Crime and Punishment, p. 260

Apple cofounder Steve Jobs loathed simple anything. That plainly helped explain his disgust with Windows. As Walter Isaacson reported in his biography of Jobs, he viewed Windows as "An inferior product."[1] Talking about Bill Gates, Jobs acidly observed that "Bill is unimaginative and has never invented anything."[2]

His biographer in Isaacson seems attracted to those operating off the beaten path in a Dostoevskian sense. To read the Russian novelist and his fascination with the visionaries, whose contrarian thoughts are so instrumental in shaping future, presently calcified thought, it's difficult to not think of people like Elon Musk and Jobs. Without minimizing Bill Gates's accomplishments for even a second in meeting and creating the needs of most computer users, that could never have been Jobs. He embodies this book's argument in the introduction that entrepreneurialism isn't a choice; rather, it's a state of mind.

Jobs was going to *lead* thinking and needs, not give people what they *thought* they wanted. As Isaacson did in fact observe about Jobs, "he acted as if he were not subject to the strictures around him."[3] This included market research so popular then and now. The "know your customer" nonsense that all too many people in all walks of life—from business to politics to technology—abide. Meeting needs or perceived needs. Telling people what they want to hear. Jobs this was not. Isaacson quotes Jobs as saying that ahead of product launches there would be no market research "because customers don't know what they want until we've shown them." Amen.

Important about the "criminal" element so eager to express something at odds with accepted wisdom, it's crucial that this state of mind be fed in the investment, and yes, thought sense. Which is why it's such a relief that Jobs's ancestors loved themselves enough to get to the United States. Really, what a tragedy it would have been for all of humankind if Jobs had been brought up in Syria, or if immigration laws had kept Musk stuck in South Africa. Per the Dostoevsky line that begins this book's concluding chapter, thank goodness for those who have a gift of talent for doing and saying something new. Immigrants frequently willing to risk it all for something better in many ways embody what Dostoevsky wrote.

Jobs's Apple Computer is a good way to begin the final chapter of *The Deficit Delusion* for so many reasons, but most notably because Apple's path underscores one of this book's foremost points that debt is a consequence of prosperity, not a signal of looming crisis as budgetary experts very much *on the beaten path* of economic thought assert with great frequency.

Traveling back in time to the 1970s, Jobs, who was rather desperate for funding, offered a New York City computer store owner 10 percent of Apple Computer for $10,000.[4] The reality is that Jobs and cofounder Steve Wozniak didn't really have many choices. The market for original thought is generally small to nonexistent. When Jobs wanted to meet with Silicon Valley VC legends Tom Perkins and Eugene Kleiner, they refused the meeting. Bill Draper, another VC pioneer, initially sent an associate over to see him.

Eventually Mike Markkula, who'd made it big on Intel stock options, went to visit with Jobs in what Sebastian Mallaby reports was his "suburban garage, the modest structure that would later inspire waves of tech startups."[5] What's important for the purposes of this book is that Markkula was able to secure for himself 26 *percent* of Apple for $91,000. Stop and contemplate this. The man who will go down as the Thomas Edison of his time, the visionary who brought so much technological elegance to the world, had to give up over a quarter of his creation for $91,000.

Oh my, is capital ever expensive! This is particularly true for Dostoevskian figures like Jobs operating so counter to conventional wisdom. Capital was expensive because Jobs was going so very much against the grain. Apple's initial valuation was $5,309, but in December 1980 when it went public (the most oversubscribed IPO since Ford Motor Co. in 1956), Apple achieved a valuation of *$1.79 billion*. Over three hundred people would become millionaires on the day of the IPO, and Jobs himself was suddenly worth $256 million.[6] Why was Jobs so rich? *Clown question*, you might say, but the better answer can be found in the discussion of Phil Knight from chapter 2. Jobs's wealth was rooted in the utter outlandishness of his vision. Particularly in the early days, few saw the future that Jobs saw, as evidenced by his desperate search for buyers of shares in a company once valued a little over $5,000.

Where the Apple story becomes most pertinent to this book comes upon Jobs's return to the company from exile in 1997. Apple was in desperate shape. Jobs harshly observed that "The products *suck*! There's no sex in them anymore."[7] Worse, the company was in serious financial trouble, no doubt at least somewhat as a consequence of the lousy products. Though Jobs laid off over 3,000 employees, he later told

Isaacson that "We were less than ninety days from being insolvent."[8] Yes, the notion of "easy money" so popular among ordinary economists and pundits is so totally at odds with reality. Particularly those frothing at the mouth to say something new.

As of the end of 1998 Apple had debt of $954 million that was largely run up by the previous regime. Worse, Apple's debt had been downgraded to junk status as a reflection of market skepticism about its ability to pay monies owed back. Really, how easily we forget how little consensus there was that Jobs would turn the company around. "What would I do? I'd shut it down and give the money back to shareholders." That's what Michael Dell had said about a near-bankrupt Apple in 1997.

Yet as readers already know, Jobs achieved a remarkable turnaround. By 2004, and after a number of successful product launches like the iMac and iPod, Apple paid off its debts, only for Jobs to exult that "Today is a historic day of sorts for our company."[9]

Considering Apple twenty years after it paid off its debts, what would you the reader guess its debts are now? Keep in mind that Apple went from near bankruptcy in the late 1990s with under a billion in debt, but now it can claim a valuation of roughly $3.3 trillion. And with valuations but a projection of all the dollars a company will earn in all its existence, it's no surprise that Apple can presently claim over $100 billion in debt. As is the case with individuals, businesses, and governments, those with lots of wealth, incoming earnings, and the expectation of much greater earnings in the future, can borrow with ease.

Really, the world is not very complicated. For the well-to-do, borrowing is simple, for those who aren't, borrowing is difficult to nonexistent. Money is the opposite of dumb.

Why all these business examples throughout a book ostensibly about government debt? The obvious answer is that the ease with which successful corporations borrow versus start-ups that can't borrow on the very best days makes the crucial point about how ruthless money is. But it's more than that.

The goal in showing how corporations have gone from all equity finance (if they were lucky) to easy borrowing amid soaring valuations hopefully conveys to readers this crucial truth: the ease with which governments borrow isn't due to money printing, or generous central banks, or due to luck; rather, it's a loud signal of how much the rich in the United States are wildly overtaxed. Governments have no resources. They can only borrow insofar as they arrogate to themselves the wealth of the rich.

In other words, money and borrowing is easy for governments precisely because they have taxable access to the wealth of individuals like Jobs, Musk, Bezos, and others for whom money was anything but "easy" on their path to wealth. Since entrepreneurs are striving to invent an all-new future, those with title to money must be ruthless with them. Equity finance only, if that.

Yet governments borrow with ease, and at the lowest of rates simply because on the rare occasion that opposite thinkers hit it big, long-fingered governments step in to take their cut. The hope is that readers see the obvious problem here.

Exactly because money is ruthless, it's also precious. And when governments tax and borrow, they extract what the enterprising would give anything to attain. As readers may remember from chapter 2, Phil Knight used to "pray" for liquidity so desperate was he in hot pursuit of what was so elusive.

It brings to mind a question, what's the better economic scenario for the United States: $1 trillion in annual debt on $1.5 trillion in total federal spending, or $7.5 trillion in annual spending, but the budget in balance? Sorry, but *clown question*. The problem is that the answer would plainly not be simple to the conventional in economic thought and the debt and deficit hawks featured throughout this book.

So wrong are the hawks about the alleged problem of debt that they can't possibly see what readers who grasp this book will see is an obvious answer. That the deficit scenario mentioned above would vastly exceed the "balanced budget" one is screamingly obvious.

The simple, nearly always glossed over truth in economics is that the weird focus among economists, pundits, and politicians on taxing vs. borrowing by governments amounts to making a distinction where there is none. The economic sin is in the extraction of precious wealth, not how it's extracted. The more wealth taken from the private sector by grasping governments, the much less that those way outside the proverbial lines, but who actually have something new to say, get to say whatever it is they want to say.

Let's never forget that these Dostoevskian thinkers are likely to fail, and they do fail over 90 percent of the time. But that's why it's so essential that they be heard. Intent on taking us in all new directions, they increase the knowledge that is wealth regardless of whether they succeed or not. Contrast this with those who are trying to meet our needs by pursuing what is already known. Even if they succeed, we haven't learned much.

Please keep this in mind as left, right, and in-between all tell you that the crisis of government consumption is tomorrow's problem, born of markets finally getting wise to governments and cutting them off. It would be difficult to happen on a more obtuse, progress-crushing way of looking at the world, yet as this book has hopefully revealed with great repetition, it's how left, right and in-between view the deficits and debt: that the problems still await. They loom. The crisis is ahead. No, not at all.

The crisis is in the extraction as governments with taxable access to the wealth creation of intrepid, opposite-thinking creators for whom capital was never easy, tax and borrow with ease. They then consume these precious resources on the known, burdened by the ordinary thoughts in their head which ensure they'll never pursue the unknown ideas that populate the minds of true entrepreneurs.

Yes, the deficit scenario that begins this discussion is unquestionably the correct scenario precisely because the scenario involves quite a bit less extraction of precious resources from the private sector. Basic common sense. Except that it's not.

As evidenced by the beliefs expressed by budgetary experts across the ideological spectrum, the routinely suggested real problem is the debt born of governments "spending beyond their means." About this point of view, it's led to more than a few debates between your author and the great libertarian economist, George Mason University professor Don Boudreaux. Boudreaux doesn't share the view of your author, that the deficit vs. "balanced budget" is "a clown question."

Boudreaux has long made a case that the truly "immoral" act is to leave debt behind to future generations, to the "grandchildren" as it were. He also thinks I'm wrong every bit as passionately as I think I'm right. And as the quotations of eminent thinkers from prominent think tanks, newspapers, and politics reveal, the consensus favors Boudreaux. According to accepted wisdom, the crisis still awaits in the form of nominally high debt that the proverbial grandchildren will "inherit."

Could Boudreaux be persuaded? To answer the question brings to mind a quip from the great essayist Joseph Epstein, that he's never lost an argument, but he's also never won an argument. Which is why I'll speculate that if presented with this book's arguments, the gracious Boudreaux would scoff.

Still, it would be nice to persuade him simply because it might surprise him that I share his view about the immorality of burdening the "grandchildren" with mistakes from the present. The only difference is that much more burdensome than debt left for future generations is government itself. In other words, the truly immoral inheritance is the size of government handed down to the unsuspecting. Think about it.

The debt is the easy part. Precisely because Americans are so productive, and because technological advances mean their productivity will soar to previously unimaginable heights in the future (see Chapter Nine), the inheritance of debt is simple. Conversely, government grows and grows, and as we've learned from monstrosities like Medicare and Social Security, the only limit to government growth is wealth creation.

Which is why the deficit scenario is once again so obviously the superior scenario. The simple truth is that deficits don't matter, and neither do "balanced budgets." What matters is how much wealth is being extracted from the private sector, simply because a dollar spent today, whether in deficit or in budgetary balance is the real burden for the grandchildren as needless programs are funded, only for them to grow and grow, and in the process of growing attract constituencies that ensure their permanence.

Which brings us to the other cruel inheritance for the grandchildren: a much less evolved society, one cruelly warped by the prodigals in government. As evidenced by how much the opposite in thought can occasionally achieve with the relatively microscopic amounts of capital matched with them, wealth born of information creation is precious. The burden for our theoretical grandchildren isn't debt; rather, it's the extraction of precious wealth that will be consumed rather than matched with "borderline crazy" minds intent on inventing an all-new and much better future.

So yes, it is immoral to burden future generations with the errors of the present, but the burden isn't debt; instead, it's the size of government that future generations must inherit paired with the problems that won't be solved and the frontiers that won't be crossed because the government taxed and borrowed so much from the productive. Say it over and over again that deficits and debt are but symptoms of the real problem, which is too much tax revenue for the federal government now, and the expectation of exponentially more tax revenue for the federal government in the future.

Yet this problem of too much tax revenue now and way too much tax revenue in the future has no currency in the policy discussions.

And since it doesn't, since the experts aren't seeing the real problem, they can't have real discussions of how to fix the problem. Asked bluntly, how can they fix a problem that they so plainly don't understand? From MacGuineas to Riedl to Rampell to Galston to Bourne to Boccia, and so many more, the inevitable answer from each is taxation sufficient to generate more tax revenue.

Sadly, the discussion doesn't appear poised for a change anytime soon. Evidence supporting this claim can be found in a *Washington Post* editorial from July 2024, and that made mention of a "new project" launched by the Peter G. Peterson Foundation. The editorial reported that the foundation "asked seven think tanks from across the ideological spectrum to submit detailed plans for putting the debt back on a sustainable trajectory." Meet the new debt plan. Is it the same as the old debt plan? Well, yes. Sadly.

As the editorial went on to report, "Every single institution agreed that American borrowing must be reined in."[10] Which means every plan from every think tank across the ideological happened on symptoms of too much tax revenue now and way too much tax revenue in the future, and facile solutions to the problem in the form of Social Security "reforms," as opposed to the real problem. In other words, the project overseen by the Peterson Foundation failed before it started simply because the terms of deficit and debt discussion remain hopelessly wrongheaded.

We know this because not one think tank stated the obvious, that government borrowing in nominally massive amounts is a consequence of too much government revenue now, and the expectation of a great deal more government revenue in the future. Since no think tank, or economist, or politician, or pundit understands the true cause of all the deficits and debts, they can't possibly offer solutions that make any sense.

What about Elon Musk and "DOGE"? It's evidence that Musk's highly original business mind doesn't translate to public policy. As with the think tank crowd Musk imagines smaller government can be achieved with spending cuts, which means Musk will fail. His solutions imply that we have a spending problem when in fact we have a revenue problem. Which means best-case-scenario spending cuts will perilously free up dollars for even worse ideas dreamed up by a U.S. political class that will get to fund those ideas in perpetuity given the broadly accepted belief in policy circles that no matter what, federal tax revenue must continue to increase.

Which means government continues to grow and debt continues to grow. Why shouldn't both? If the ever-suggested "fix" for ever-growing debt is more tax revenue and more reform—measures that so clearly enable more borrowing—it seems the problem won't be solved. Hence, this book.

Addressing the actual problem of too much tax revenue now and the expectation of exponentially more tax revenues in the future, the hope here is that a few readers will be persuaded. It only takes a few to change the conversation. Because until people recognize that we have a too-much-tax-revenue problem precisely because the rich in the United States are wildly overtaxed, and that deficits and debt are a symptom of this sad fact, there will never be progress when it comes to shrinking government and its borrowing.

—John Tamny
Bethesda, MD
April 26, 2024

Acknowledgments

I'll start with Bob Reingold, the person to whom this book is dedicated. To know me is to know that I reference Bob with great regularity. He's taught me so much about business and life. And since life is economics, he's taught me a great deal about economics. Rare does a day go by where I don't think about something wise Bob has said to me, only to apply it to something I'm doing at the Parkview Institute, with family members, and with my writing. I'm very grateful for Bob, and that's quite the understatement.

As with so many people who've had a huge influence on me, I know Bob thanks to Cato Institute cofounder Ed Crane. Ed's a fellow left-hander who thinks neither right nor left, plus Ed has taught me how to think. So much of what's in this book has Ed's fingerprints and philosophy all over it.

Howie Rich interviewed me when Ed was considering hiring me at the Cato Institute back in 2003. Howie, much like Ed, is the definition of *doer*. And in doing, he's taught me a lot about what matters. I'm so glad to have his support, and just as important, his ideas.

Hall McAdams is someone I met thanks to Ed back in 2003. What a remarkable influence Hall has been. So much of what I write and say is a consequence of conversations conducted with Hall over the years.

I'm proud to say he's on the board of the Parkview Institute. I'm also glad to welcome Trish, Hall's wife, into a future of lengthy discussions meant to solve the world's problems.

Richard Masson first took a meeting with me in 2003. Much as Hall did, Richard treated me as a thinker with occasionally worthwhile thoughts even though my bio then was "a writer in Washington, D.C." At risk of getting all Irish (a term lifted from Hall) on both, their interest in what I had to say back when no one was interested gave me confidence when there was little reason for me to be confident.

Which brings up the great Steve Forbes. Ever since his run for president in 1996, and certainly before that, I'd admired him from afar. And read him closely. To then have him quote me out of the blue in 2005, in *Fact and Comment* no less, was one of the most exciting things that ever happened to me. Steve could have so easily just referenced my thinking without mentioning me, but incredibly generous person that he is, he chose to help someone who really needed the help. I'm forever grateful to him.

Bob Landry is the other board member at Parkview, which means I get to occupy much more of his time than I otherwise have the chance to. Bob is so wise, and such a great person to talk contrarian policy with. I always tell him, and he agrees, that a very small room would fit the people who think as we do. After that, Bob is such an uplifting source of encouragement. Bob knows arguably more than anyone how routinely my op-eds and books are criticized, only for him to regularly step in and support me.

I know Bob through Rafe Resendes, the cofounder of Applied Finance Group (AFG). As with so many of the people mentioned here, Rafe took me seriously when no one seemingly would. I very much wanted to present my frequently contrarian ideas with investors and thinkers, and Rafe emailed me in 2006 to ask me to speak in Las Vegas to his AFG clients. It was a big deal then, and it still very much is.

Charlie Sauer and Norm Singleton are my colleagues at the Market Institute. Each time I speak with Charlie we marvel at how lucky we are to do what we do. Some people say the market liberal side of the economics discussion is the difficult side to take. Charlie and I know better. Much better.

Jon Decker, Phil Bell, and Rob Smith are my Parkview Institute colleagues. I'm very lucky to work with them. They're so energetic and optimistic, and they're both because they're muscular believers in what we're doing. Our aim isn't to convince people of the genius of free markets. We don't need to. Ed Crane, Howie Rich, Steve Forbes, and others like them won that debate back in the 1980s. And they won big. What Decker, Bell, Smith and I are trying to do is improve the discussion of a subject that's still stalked by fallacy despite the market-liberal side having won. We think if we can improve the terms of the discussion just a little, that economic growth and opportunity will grow by a lot.

Big thanks go to A. J. Rice for connecting me with, or better yet, reconnecting me with Regnery Publishing. I always enjoy working with them, and this time was no exception. Thank you very much to Tony Lyons, president of Skyhorse Publishing (owner of Regnery), and Isaac Morris for his excellent and encouraging edit. Isaac could have easily cut, cut, and cut some more given how at odds the book's ideas are with conventional thought, but instead he chose to approach my thoughts with an open mind.

It goes without saying how thankful I am for my parents, Peter and Nancy. My mother, like me, is left-handed. Crane tells me left-handers are different and think differently. I think he's correct. Which means I'm grateful to my mom for passing on to me a genetic oddity that frequently reveals itself in opposite viewpoints, and I'm grateful to my dad for imbuing within me the inclination to question everything. Thank you to my sister Kim for being such a great sister and, if possible, a much better aunt.

Which brings me to my wife Kendall, and kids, Claire and Reed (a.k.a. Wiggles). It would certainly be politic to say that without Kendall there would be no books, but in her case, I can say it because it's true. Kendall is my purpose, inspiration, and crucially at times, my critic. She long ago demanded more of me than I was demanding of myself, and I'm so thankful for that. I'm equally grateful that she brought Reed and Claire into the world. Like Kendall, they're my purpose and inspiration, and increasingly my sounding boards. I can't wait to see what we four accomplish in the future.

Endnotes

Introduction

1. Richard Rubin & Xavier Martinez, "The Best Things In Life—And Presidential Campaigns—Are Free," *Wall Street Journal*, October 15, 2024
2. Holman Jenkins, "The Veeps Were San on Climate," *Wall Street Journal*, October 9, 2024
3. Editorial, "When will the national debt hit the campaign trail?" *Washington Post*, September 16, 2024
4. Jaqueline Alemany & Matt Viser, "Trump gives Musk his full support," *Washington Post*, February 27, 2025
5. Sebastian Mallaby, *The Power Law*, Penguin Random House, 2022, p. 352
6. Jimmy Soni, *The Founders*, Simon & Schuster, 2022, p. xvi
7. Clifford Asness, Capitalism Is the Real Target, *Commentary Magazine*, July/August 2024
8. Fyodor Dostoevsky, *Crime and Punishment*, Alfred A. Knopf, 1993, p. 260
9. John Mackey, *The Whole Story*, Matt Holt, 2024, p. 4
10. Ibid., *The Whole Story*, p. 51
11. Fyodor Dostoevsky, *Crime and Punishment*, Alfred A. Knopf, 1993, p. 261
12. Ibid., *The Whole Story*, p. 156
13. Sebastian Mallaby, *The Power Law*, Penguin Random House, 2022, p. 114
14. Ibid., *The Power Law*, p. 9

15　Ibid., *The Power Law*, p. 198
16　Ibid., *The Power Law*, p. 211
17　Ibid., *The Power Law*, p. 211
18　Ibid., *The Power Law*, p. 3

Chapter One

1　Steven Witt, "How Jensen Huang's Nvidia Is Powering the A.I. Revolution," *The New Yorker*, November 27, 2023
2　Ben Cohen, "The 84-Year Old Man Who Saved Nvidia," *Wall Street Journal*, May 18, 2024
3　Jacob Bogage, "National debt will hit $50.7 trillion by 2034, federal budget agency projects," *Washington Post*, June 19, 2024
4　Andrew Wilford, "Addressing Paul Krugman's Case Against Debt Worry," RealClearMarkets, June 18, 2024
5　Ryan Bourne, "Krugman's Cold Comfort On the Federal Debt," *Cato Institute*, June 13, 2024
6　Catherine Rampell, "Our borrowing might finally come back to bite us," *Washington Post*, October 6, 2023
7　Richard M. Salsman, *The Political Economy of the Public Debt*, Edward Elgar Publishing, 2017, p. 25
8　Editorial, "On the debt, the U.S. faces a leadership deficit, too." *Washington Post*, June 21, 2024
9　Editorial, "Soaring U.S. Debt Is a Spending Problem," *Wall Street Journal*, June 20, 2024
10　William A. Galston, "The National Debt Crisis Is Coming," *Wall Street Journal*, June 26, 2024
11　Brian Riedl, "Debt will hit a shocking $50 trillion by 2034," *New York Post*, June 19, 2024

Chapter Two

1　John Tamny, "Mark Steyn Resides In a Crowded—And Centuries Old—Echo Chamber of American Doom," *Forbes*, October 28, 2013
2　Phil Knight, *Shoe Dog*, Scribner, 2016, p. 160

3   Bret Stephens, How Capitalism Went Off Of the Rails, *New York Times*, June 18, 2024
4   Phil Knight, *Shoe Dog*, Scribner, 2016, p. 160
5   Richard M. Salsman, *The Political Economy of the Public Debt*, Edward Elgar Publishing, 2017, pp. 60–61
6   Ibid., p. 70
7   Ibid., p. 71
8   Ibid., p. 61
9   William A. Galston, "The National Debt Crisis Is Coming," *Wall Street Journal*, June 26, 2024
10 Ryan Bourne, "Krugman's Cold Comfort On the Federal Debt," *Cato Institute*, June 13, 2024
11 Catherine Rampell, "How much did Congress lose by defunding the IRS? Way more than we thought." *Washington Post*, June 14, 2023
12 Donald Luskin, "Smells Like Victory," *National Review Online*, July 12, 2005

Chapter Three

1   Robert H. Smith, *Dead Bank Walking*, Oakhill Press, 1995, pp. 58–68
2   Catherine Rampell, "Two myths about Trump's civil-fraud trial," *Washington Post*, March 25, 2024
3   Dan Mitchell, The Looming Fiscal Crisis, *International Liberty*, June 23, 2024
4   Jacob Bogage, "Election result likely to affect ballooning debt," *Washington Post*, June 27, 2024

Chapter Four

1   Bernie Marcus and Arthur Blank, *Built From Scratch*, Times Business/Random House, 1999, p. 50
2   Ibid., p. xvi
3   David Bahnsen, *Full-Time: Work and the Meaning of Life*, Post Hill Press, 2024.
4   David Bahnsen, *Full-Time*
5   Bernie Marcus and Arthur Blank, *Built From Scratch*, Times Business/Random House, 1999 p. 38

6   Lawrence Summers, "The Biden stimulus is admirably ambitious. But it brings some big risks too," *Washington Post*, February 4, 2021
7   Phil Gramm and Mike Solon, "The Democrats' Inflation Blame Game," *Wall Street Journal*, January 12, 2022
8   Jeanna Smialek, "Eager for Vacation? Some Pull Back as Income Gap Swells," *New York Times*, July 4, 2024
9   Bernie Marcus and Arthur Blank, *Built From Scratch*, Times Business/Random House, 1999, p. 70
10 Richard Rahn, "Hard economic lessons from Germany that Americans seem to have forgotten," *Washington Times*, May 13, 2024
11 Richard Rahn, "How To Stop Inflation," *Washington Times*, November 14, 2022
12 John Cochrane, "Inflation: No Mystery Here," *Hoover Digest*, Winter 2024
13 John Cochrane, "What We've Learned About Inflation," *Wall Street Journal*, August 1, 2023
14 Niall Ferguson, *The Cash Nexus*, Basic Books, 2001, p. 197
15 Richard M. Salsman, *The Political Economy of the Public Debt*, Edward Elgar Publishing, 2017, p. 20
16 Niall Ferguson, *The Cash Nexus*, Basic Books, 2001, p. 172
17 Bernie Marcus and Arthur Blank, *Built From Scratch*, Times Business/Random House, 1999, p. 51
18 Christopher Leonard, *The Lords of Easy Money*, Simon & Schuster, 2022, p. 131
19 Walter Isaacson, *Elon Musk*, Simon & Schuster, 2023, p. 277
20 Walter Isaacson, *Elon Musk*, Simon & Schuster, 2023, pp. 178–79
21 Christopher Leonard, *The Lords of Easy Money*, Simon & Schuster, 2022, p. 131
22 Steven Rattner, "Voodoo Economics, Then and Now," *New York Times*, May 2, 2017
23 Megan McArdle, "It's getting harder for states to find the income-tax sweet spot," *Washington Post*, February 21, 2024
24 Stephen Moore, "Reaganomics Won the Day," *National Review Online*, June 7, 2004
25 Walter Isaacson, *Elon Musk*, Simon & Schuster, 2023, p. 278

Chapter Six

1. David Asman, "The Mobile Guide: Artistes and Apparatchiks," *Wall Street Journal*, August 12, 1992
2. Anton Troianovski & Patrick Kingsley, "Russians Who Want To Be Anywhere But Russia," *New York Times*, March 14, 2022
3. Anna Fifield, *The Great Successor*, PublicAffairs, 2019, p. 148
4. Virginia Lopez Glass, "Virginia's New Lettuce-Based Economy Is Good Enough For Now," *New York Times*, September 6, 2021
5. Farnaz Fassihi, "With Inflation Ravaging Currency, Iran Is Replacing Names and Numbers," *New York Times*, May 4, 2020
6. Jorg Guido Hulsmann, "The Cultural and Political Consequences of Fiat Money," Mises Institute, November 20, 2014
7. Daphne Posadas, "Argentina's Recent Inflation Trends Are Proving Hazlitt Right," Foundation for Economic Education, July 2, 2024
8. Veronique de Rugy, "The National Debt Is Crossing An Ominous Line," *Reason*, July 4, 2024
9. Walter Isaacson, *Elon Musk*, Simon & Schuster, 2023, p. 409

Chapter Seven

1. Reggie Ugwu, "Michael Jackson Died With More Than $500 Million in Debt," *New York Times*, July 1, 2024
2. George Gilder, *Life After Capitalism*, Regnery Gateway, 2023, p. 7
3. George Gilder, *Life After Capitalism*, Regnery Gateway, 2023, p. 5
4. David McCullough, *The Wright Brothers*, Simon & Schuster, 2015, p. 34
5. David McCullough, *The Wright Brothers*, Simon & Schuster, 2015, p. 33
6. Adam Smith, *The Wealth of Nations*, Scribner's Modern Library, p. 377
7. Adam Smith, *The Wealth of Nations*, Scribner's Modern Library, p. 368
8. Source: Flemming v. Nestor, Supreme Court
9. Peter Baker & Susan Glasser, *The Man Who Ran Washington*, Doubleday, 2020, p. 166
10. Ben Cohen, "He Made His Office a Monument to Failure," *Wall Street Journal*, July 20–21, 2024

11 George Gilder, *Life After Capitalism*, Regnery Gateway, 2023, p. 36
12 Walter Isaacson, *Elon Musk*, Simon & Schuster, 2023, p. 123
13 Walter Isaacson, *Elon Musk*, Simon & Schuster, 2023, p. 153
14 Walter Isaacson, *Elon Musk*, Simon & Schuster, 2023, p. 390
15 Walter Isaacson, *Elon Musk*, Simon & Schuster, 2023, p. 187
16 Ashlee Vance, *Elon Musk*, Ecco, 2015, p. 215
17 Daniel Gilbert, "A paralyzed man walks with brain and spine implants," *Washington Post*, May 24, 2023
18 Romina Boccia, "From Debt Ceiling Crisis to Debt Crisis," Cato Institute, May 22, 2023

Chapter Eight

1 Editorial, "California Gets Another Budget Deficit Shock," *Wall Street Journal*, February 21, 2024
2 Reis Thebault, "How California's $100 billion surplus became a 'budget emergency,'" *Washington Post*, June 23, 2024
3 George Will, "Democrats, fear not an open convention," *Washington Post*, July 22, 2024
4 Source: Statista, https://www.statista.com/statistics/305287/california-state-debt/#:~:text=In%20the%20fiscal%20year%20of,Stated%20can%20be%20found%20ohere.
5 Lee Ohanian, "Newsom Wants to Add $6.4 Billion to California's $1.6 Trillion Debt With Proposition 1," Hoover Institution, February 13, 2024
6 Walter Isaacson, *The Innovators*, Simon & Schuster, 2014, p. 185
7 Sebastian Mallaby, *The Power Law*, Penguin Random House, 2022, p. 26
8 Michael Freeman, *ESPN: The Uncensored History*, Taylor Trade Publishing, 2000, p. 49
9 Warrren Brookes, *The Economy In Mind*, Universe Books, 1982, p. 55
10 Editorial, "The U.S. Already Soaks the Rich," *Wall Street Journal*, March 29, 2024
11 Glenn Kessler, "Biden keeps saying billionaires pay 8 percent in federal taxes. Not really." *Washington Post*, January 28, 2024
12 Sebastian Mallaby, *The Power Law*, Penguin Random House, 2022, p. 391

13 Editorial, "California Gets Another Budget Deficit Shock," *Wall Street Journal*, February 21, 2024
14 Reis Thebault, "How California's $100 billion surplus became a 'budget emergency,'" *Washington Post*, June 23, 2024
15 George Gilder, *Life After Capitalism*, Regnery Gateway, 2023, p. 7
16 Dan Mitchell, "The Unavoidable Choice: Entitlement Reform or Massive Middle-Class Tax Increases," International Liberty, December 22, 2022

Chapter Nine

1 Paolo Confino, "Could AI create a one-person unicorn? Sam Altman thinks so—and Silicon Valley sees the technology waiting for us," *Fortune*, February 4, 2024
2 Chip Cutter, "AI Is Taking on New Work," *Wall Street Journal*, March 10, 2024
3 Steven Watts, The People's Tycoon, Alfred A. Knopf, 2005, p. 119
4 Faye Bowers, "Building a 747: 43 Days and 3 Million Fasteners," *Christian Science Monitor*, October 29, 1997
5 Bret Stephens, "Other People's Babies," *Wall Street Journal*, March 21, 2017
6 Dan Mitchell, "In One Image: Everything You Need to Know about America's Demographic Challenge," *International Liberty*, August 26, 2015
7 Dan Mitchell, "Demographic Doom and the Welfare State," *International Liberty*, September 23, 2023
8 Rep. David Schweikert, "Congress has an obligation to restore nation's fiscal health. Here's how it can," The Hill, July 1, 2024
9 Catherine Rampell, "Americans are having too few kids. The GOP made the problem worse," *Washington Post*, May 1, 2024
10 Monica Hesse, "Don't blame birth givers for the birth rate," *Washington Post*, June 27, 2024
11 Natalie Robehmed, "At 21, Kylie Jenner Becomes the Youngest Self-Made Billionaire Ever," *Forbes*, July 11, 2018
12 Natalie Robehmed, "How 20-Year Old Kylie Jenner Built a $900 Million *Fortune* in Less than Three Years, " *Forbes*, July 11, 2018
13 Dan Mitchell, "Chinese Economic Policy, Part I: The Demographic Challenge," *International Liberty*, July 16, 2024

14 Eswar Prasad, *The Future of Money*, Harvard University Press, p. 75
15 Michael Breen, *The New Koreans*, Thomas Dunne Books, 2017, p. 78
16 Michael Breen, *The New Koreans*, Thomas Dunne Books, 2017, p. 76
17 Lawrence Dorr, *Die Once, Live Twice*, Silverado Books, 2011, p. 129
18 Gerry Shih & Karishma Mehrotra, "India's population overtakes China's, but numbers mask a bigger story," *Washington Post*, April 14, 2023

Chapter Ten

1 John Tierney, "The March of Dimes Syndrome," *City Journal*, Spring 2024
2 Ryan Bourne, "Five Fiscal Truths," Cato at Liberty, April 18, 2024
3 Editorial, "One speech, two Mr. Trumps," *Washington Post*, July 21, 2024
4 Brian Riedl, "Why Did Americans Stop Caring About the National Debt?", *Reason Magazine*, August/September 2024
5 Kristen Welker, Allan Smith, Sahil Kapur, Yamiche Alcindor, and Matt Dixon, "Trump allies press the White House to dial back Elon Musk's media interviews over his Social Security jabs," NBC News, March 23, 2025
6 Brian Riedl, "Why Did Americans Stop Caring About the National Debt?", *Reason Magazine*, August/September 2024
7 Dan Mitchell, "The Unavoidable Choice: Entitlement Reform or Massive Middle-Class Tax Increases," International Liberty, December 22, 2022
8 Ryan Bourne, "Five Fiscal Truths," Cato at Liberty, April 18, 2024
9 Romina Boccia, "From Debt Ceiling Crisis to Debt Crisis," Cato Institute, May 22, 2023
10 Source: Yahoo Finance
11 Stephen Moore, "Do the rich pay their fair share?" The Heritage Foundation, March 3, 2015
12 Steven F. Hayward, *The Age of Reagan: The Fall of the Old Liberal Order, 1964–80*, Prima Publishing, 2001, p. 19
13 Sally C. Pipes, "Medicare at 50: Hello, Mid-Life Crisis," *Wall Street Journal*, July 30, 2015
14 Romina Boccia, "National Security Implications of Unsustainable Spending and Debt," Cato at Liberty, July 27, 2023

15 Catherine Rampell, "Why we're borrowing to fund the elderly while neglecting everyone else," *Washington Post*, November 21, 2023
16 Catherine Rampell, "Our borrowing might finally come back to bite us," *Washington Post*, October 6, 2023
17 Jeff Stein, "U.S. payments on debt spike to $659 billion, nearly doubling in two years," *Washington Post*, October 21, 2023
18 Holman Jenkins, "The U.S. Needs a Defense Buildup," *Wall Street Journal*, October 11, 2023
19 Jacob Bogage, "National debt will hit $50.7 trillion by 2034, federal budget agency projects," *Washington Post*, June 19, 2024

Conclusion

1 Walter Isaacson, *Steve Jobs*, Simon & Schuster, p. 295
2 Walter Isaacson, *Steve Jobs*, Simon & Schuster, p. 172
3 Walter Isaacson, *Steve Jobs*, Simon & Schuster, p. 119
4 Sebastian Mallaby, *The Power Law*, Penguin Random House, 2022, p. 82
5 Sebastian Mallaby, *The Power Law*, Penguin Random House, 2022, p. 84
6 Walter Isaacson, *Steve Jobs*, Simon & Schuster, pp. 102–4
7 Walter Isaacson, *Steve Jobs*, Simon & Schuster, p. 317
8 Walter Isaacson, *Steve Jobs*, Simon & Schuster, p. 339
9 Evan Niu, "16 Years After Freeing Itself from Debt, Apple Now Owes over $100 Billion," The Motley Fool, February 20, 2020
10 Editorial, "The national debt can be tamed," *Washington Post*, July 24, 2024

Index

A

AI. *See* artificial intelligence (AI)
Altman, Sam, 107, 109, 116
Amazon, xii–xiii. *See also* Bezos, Jeff
Apple Computer, 132–134
Argentina, 66–67, 71–75
artificial intelligence (AI), 1, 108–109
Asman, David, 63–64
Auerbach, Alan, ix
Austrian School, 66–67, 73, 99

B

Bahnsen, David, 37, 39, 45
Baker, James A., 88
Baker, Peter, 88, 119
Bandow, Doug, 18–19
Benchmark Capital, xii, xiii, xix
Bernanke, Ben, 49–50

Bezos, Jeff, xiii, 112
Biden, Joe, 38–39, 97, 101, 121
birthrates, 109–110, 113–114
Blank, Arthur, 35–38, 47
Boccia, Romina, 93–94, 122, 126–127
Boudreaux, Don, 137
Bourne, Ryan, 5–6, 20, 95, 120–122
Brookes, Warren, 1–2, 97
Built from Scratch (Marcus and Blank), 36

C

California, 97–99, 102–103
Carville, James, 129
Cheney, Dick, 57
China, 112–113, 116
Cochrane, John, 41, 47
Cohen, Ben, 2

Coolidge, Calvin, 100
Crime and Punishment (Dostoevsky), ix, 131

D
debt crisis, xx–xxi, 25, 75, 93, 95, 121
de Rugy, Veronique, 75–76, 105
DOGE (Department of Government Efficiency), xi, 121, 139–140
dollar, 44–45, 63–64, 72
Dostoevsky, Fyodor, ix, xiv, 83, 131
Draper, Bill, 133

E
Economy in Mind, The (Brookes), 1, 97
election of 2024, ix–xii
entrepreneurialism, xiv–xviii, 1–2, 13–14, 29, 54, 81, 83–84, 86–87, 131, 135–136

F
Federal Reserve, 14, 49, 75–76
FEE. *See* Foundation for Economic Education (FEE)
Ferguson, Niall, 42–44, 46
fertility rates, 109–110, 113–114
Fifield, Anna, 65
Fiscal Theory of the Price Level, The (Cochrane), 41
Fisher, Richard, 49–50
Flemming v. Nestor, 125
Fonda, Jane, 118
Ford, Henry, 109
Foundation for Economic Education (FEE), 67–69, 71
Founders, The (Soni), xiii
Franklin, Benjamin, 11, 16
Full-Time (Bahnsen), 37

G
Galston, William, 9, 20, 31, 95
Gates, Bill, 131
Germany, 71–72
Gilbert, Daniel, 92
Gilder, George, 81–82, 88
Giscard d'Estaing, Valéry, 44
Glasser, Susan, 88, 119
Gramm, Phil, 39–40, 86
Greatest Ponzi Scheme on Earth, The: How the U.S. Can Avoid Economic Collapse (Rubin), 31
Great Society, 124
Gurley, Bill, xii

H
Haiti, 26, 43, 52, 105
Hamilton, Alexander, 15–16, 19
Harding, Warren, 100
Harper, Bryce, 2
Harris, Kamala, ix, 121
Hayden, Tom, 118
Heller, Walter, 123
Hesse, Monica, 111

Home Depot, 35–37, 40, 42–43, 47–48
Huang, Jensen, 2–3
Hülsmann, Guido, 66–67

I
Illinois, 105
India, 113
inflation, 35, 38–48, 67–69, 72, 75
interest rates, xvii, 12–14, 17, 28, 38, 47, 50–52, 128–129
Internal Revenue Service (IRS), 20–21, 30, 101, 104. See also taxation
Iran, 65–66
Irimajiri, Shoichiro, 3
Isaacson, Walter, 89–90, 131, 134

J
Jackson, Michael, 79–80
Jacobsohn, Sean, 88
Jefferson, Thomas, 16–17
Jenkins, Holman, x, 129
Jenner, Kylie, 111–112
Jobs, Steve, 131–134
Johnson, Lyndon B., 124
Just the Good Stuff (VandeHei), 117

K
Kalanick, Travis, xii, xiii, xvii
Kennedy, John F., 122–123
Kessler, Glenn, 100–101
Khosla, Vinod, xviii, 2, 108–109

Kim Jong-un, 65
Kleiner, Eugene, 133
Knight, Phil, 11–12, 14–15, 135
Krugman, Paul, 5, 33

L
Laffer Curve, 32, 52–53, 56–59
Langone, Ken, 35–37
Life after Capitalism (Gilder), 81, 88
Luskin, Donald, 21–22

M
Ma, Jack, 112–113, 116
MacGuineas, Maya, 4, 20, 31, 93, 122, 129–130
Mackey, John, xv–xvi
Mallaby, Sebastian, xvi, 87, 133
Manhattan Institute (MI), 6, 21, 93, 104, 117–118
March of Dimes Syndrome, 117–118
Marcus, Bernie, 35–38, 47
Markkula, Mike, 133
McArdle, Megan, 52–53, 56
McCullough, David, 83
Mead, Carver, 88–89
Medicare, 75, 87, 116, 120–125, 127–128, 130
MI. See Manhattan Institute (MI)
Milei, Javier, 67, 71–73
Mitchell, Dan, 31, 95, 104–105, 110, 112–115, 121

MMT. *See* Modern Monetary Theory (MMT)
Modern Monetary Theory (MMT), 66–67, 70, 99
"money printing," 45, 67–72, 105
Moore, Stephen, 32, 53, 57–58, 122–123
Morris, Robert, 15
Mundell, Robert, 107
Musk, Elon, xi, xvi, 50, 60, 76–77, 89–91, 121, 131–132, 139–140
MYbank, 112–113

N
Nash, Ogden, 49
Newsom, Gavin, 97–98, 102–103
Nike, 11–12, 14–15
Nixon, Richard, 44
Nock, Albert Jay, 35, 39
North Korea, 65
Nvidia, 1–3, 7–9, 13, 19

P
Parker, David, 85
Perkins, Tom, 133
Perot, Ross, 35–36, 47
Peterson, Michael, 128
Peterson Foundation, 128–129
Pipes, Sally, 124
Political Economy of Public Debt, The (Salsman), 17
Power Law, The (Mallaby), xvi

productivity, 55, 58, 81, 83, 94, 108–109, 111–113, 115, 137

R
Rahn, Richard, 31, 41, 46–47, 95
Rampell, Catherine, 6, 20–21, 29–30, 33–34, 95, 110–111, 114, 126–127
Rattner, Steven, 51–53, 56
Reagan, Ronald, 51–53, 55–57, 59–61, 98, 102, 119, 127
Riedl, Jessica, 6, 9, 20–21, 30, 95, 104, 121, 128
Riley, Talulah, 50
Rockefeller, Laurance, 99
Ruin, Les, 31
Russia, 25–26, 43, 65
ruthlessness, 27–28, 34, 56, 67, 71, 88, 106

S
Salsman, Richard, 17
Say, Jean-Baptiste, 63
Say's Law, 39
Schweikert, David, 110
Sega, 3
Sharma, Ruchir, 12–14
Smith, Adam, 23, 27–28, 64, 79, 81, 83, 85, 108–109
Smith, Robert, 26–27
Social Security, 75, 87, 116, 120–122, 124–128, 130
Soni, Jimmy, xiii

South Korea, 113
Soviet Union, 63–65
SpaceX, 89–91
spending, 5–7, 10, 15, 18, 20–21, 31–32, 38–41, 54, 58–60, 67–70, 72, 84, 89
Stephens, Bret, 110
Stutzman, Rob, 97
Summers, Lawrence, 38–40
supply-side economics, 6, 21, 32, 46, 52–58, 112, 121, 124
Switzerland, 45

T
tariffs, 15, 54–55
taxation, 15–22, 30–34, 93–95, 100–103, 119, 123. *See also* Internal Revenue Service (IRS)
tax cuts, 49–61, 100, 102, 123
Tesla, 50, 60
Texas Instruments (TI), 49–50
Thiel, Peter, xvi–xvii, 8, 82, 87, 99, 107
Tierney, John, 117–118

Trump, Donald, ix, x, 23, 26–30, 33–34, 121

U
Uber, xii, xix, 7–9, 13, 19

V
VandeHei, Jim, 117, 119

W
Warren, Elizabeth, 76–77
Wealth of Nations, The (Smith), 23, 79, 83, 108
welfare state, 110, 112–116
West Virginia, 98, 105
Whole Foods, xv–xvi
Whole Story, The (Mackey), xv
Wilford, Andrew, 5
Will, Geoge, 97
Wozniak, Steve, 132–133
Wright brothers, 82–83

Z
Zero to One (Thiel), 8, 82
Zimbabwe, 66